MEDICAL SPANISH

Real Spanish Medical Conversations
for Healthcare Professionals

www.LingoMastery.com

Free Book Reveals The 6 Step Blueprint That Took Students **From Language Learners To Fluent In 3 Months**

- **6 Unbelievable Hacks** that will accelerate your learning curve

- **Mind Training:** why memorizing vocabulary is easy

- **One Hack To Rule Them All:** This <u>secret nugget</u> will blow you away...

Head over to **LingoMastery.com/hacks**
and claim your free book now!

CONTENTS

INTRODUCTION

Hello, reader! Welcome to **Medical Spanish: Real Spanish Medical Conversations for Healthcare Professionals,** a book we've written with the intention of expanding your vocabulary in the Spanish tongue and allowing you to communicate with patients and colleagues within the magnificent world of healthcare!

There are over **570 million** Spanish speakers across the world, with **21 million** of them representing the amount of students studying Spanish as a second language. The Castilian language — as Spanish as it is originally called — is spoken as an official tongue in five continents, and it represents the second most popular language in the famously multicultural United States of America. In fact, there are over **55 million** Hispanic residents in the U.S., which makes up quite a giant amount of the total population.

Even so, you might not be convinced yet. Sure, you may be just checking this book out and haven't purchased it yet due to the common doubts that any of us can feel about getting involved with a new experience. It may not even seem *that* important to learn a new language, especially when you're too busy taking care of patients or otherwise occupying your time within a hospital or clinic.

Well, we have to break it to you right now — once you start reading this book, you are really going to realize why you'll need to learn Spanish and soon. The next few paragraphs are about to change your vision on what the knowledge of Spanish means for healthcare professionals.

A skill that saves lives

You work as the only doctor at the local hospital in a small, secluded city. The night shift has been quiet, and you start to feel that you might just get a chance to nap a while before you're needed again. Suddenly, the double doors of the emergency ward thunder open, a stretcher being hauled into the expanse of the room by a worried paramedic and a crying mother. On the stretcher is a child: the boy looks in bad shape and isn't breathing, and you cross the ward with a quick run to ask the child's mother what's going on.

1

She starts talking, terrified excitement taking control as she tells you the whole tale of how her son ended up in that state, and she repeats several words with emphasis, telling you that they are *'importante'*.

Unfortunately, you look to the paramedic and then back to the woman with confusion clear on your face. She stares at you, suddenly understanding her worst dream has come true — the doctor can't save her son because he doesn't even *know* what's going on, and that he'll never understand that a *rattlesnake* just bit him.

How did that story just make you feel? Terrible, right? Imagine, on the other hand, that you understand every single word that the grieving mother manages to tell you, and that you can now identify the venom and get the antidote ready before the venom can take the child's life? *Everything changes,* and all it took was a few hours per day for a few months, and now you have just saved a life.

Being a healthcare professional has never been easy and sometimes it can be a thankless job, but there is certainly nothing like seeing the satisfaction on a patient's face as they recover from dire circumstances and learn to feel grateful with life and with modern medicine once more.

There is nothing that feels as precious as saving a life, and we can help you do that.

Who this book is for

You may already be counting yourself off as someone who should buy this book — *I'm not a doctor*, you may think, and *I probably won't have to treat anyone of Hispanic descent anytime soon for snake bites or anything at all*.

It doesn't matter if you are a doctor or not; this book has been created for anyone in the healthcare field, regardless of their roles.

Are you a nurse and may have to treat an elderly Spanish-speaking patient soon? This book is for you, in that case. Do you work as a receptionist and have to book appointments for Hispanic patients arriving at the clinic every so often? This book is also for you. What about those men and women who work in the sales department or in pharmacies, and have to make large orders of drugs and medical equipment? Don't be surprised: this book is also for you.

Do not feel limited by the position you may have as a healthcare professional: learning Spanish will certainly bring added value to your workplace, and it will open new doors for you as a specialist in what you do. Your curriculum will not only look much more appealing for any human resources department, but you are more likely to earn a higher salary than somebody who can only speak one tongue, according to important studies.

In fact, knowing how to speak both Spanish and English may be the difference between a high-profile transfer to better facilities than your current job or watching somebody else get the position instead.

How we have structured this book for you

We have written this particular book in a way that presents each lesson like a tool that you will pick up and make use of in your advancement through the challenge that is learning Spanish.

Consisting of a series of chapters based on common situations that you will face in the field of healthcare, we have decided to present each case in the most efficient way that you will encounter: in the form of a story spoken in dialogue between two people.

Each story will tell the tale of both a patient and a doctor, a nurse and a receptionist, a pharmacist and a pharmaceutical sales director — if it exists and happens commonly in the field of healthcare, you will find it in this book.

The conversations in each chapter will be written in both Spanish and English, allowing you to verify what you already may know and study what you don't, as well as giving you an almost exact word-to-word translation (while maintaining it natural where certain exceptions must be made) of everything that is being said between both sides of the tale.

Preceding each conversation's text will be a list of vocabulary related to what you are about to read, stating a list of the most complicated or technical words you will encounter, along with both their translation into English and the way you should be pronouncing them. This list will allow you to prepare yourself for what's coming up, and find out how to master the toughest health-related terms in Spanish.

That's right, we are invested in helping you learn what you need to know, even if it means going that extra way to ensure you understood each and every word.

Finally — how to get the most out of Medical Spanish: Real Spanish Medical Conversations for Healthcare Professionals

Are you still doubtful about how this book is going to work for you? It doesn't matter: we're ready to explain.

The following book can be read by men and women of all ages and professions, and the language will never be too difficult (causing you to lose faith and give up on your learning) or too simple (and not accurately represent a take on life as a healthcare professional). We believe that anyone with enough drive and desire to learn will benefit from this particular work.

Even so, there are a few tips we can give you that will guarantee you achieve the absolute best results from your lessons with this book:

1. **Study without pressure.** At no point will we enforce a schedule or time limit for you to learn your Spanish lessons, nor are we going to sell you empty promises on how the following chapters will teach you a technical level of Spanish in 2 weeks, like many other publishing companies do. Take it easy, try to read at least one chapter at a time and dominate it before you move on. Don't be afraid to make mistakes.

2. **Make use of our audio to enhance your learning.** This book is available in an audiobook version, and you can trust that you will learn more if you decide to give it a try. The *reading-while-listening* method has been proven to achieve better results when studying a new tongue, bringing advantages such as enhancement of cognitive capacities and language fluency. This tip is more than just advertising — audiobooks are definitely an excellent option when it comes to learning!

3. **Create your own resources to boost your lessons.** Whether it's a notebook to jot notes down, a word processing document so that you can place the most important terms in, or a recording of the pronunciation of a tough word; make sure you're ready and willing to create resources for your own use. It will not only

boost your learning, but you will also have some material left lying around for when you want to teach a colleague some lessons!

4. **Find a partner or group.** You cannot underestimate the power of groups, and how studies can improve when you group up and use two minds to solve problems that one mind wouldn't have accomplished on its own. Don't be shy: there are many people who will want to practice with you and acquire their own version of *Medical Spanish: Real Spanish Medical Conversations for Healthcare Professionals,* so start practicing with a partner today and reap the benefits of group studies!

That is all, student; we have now reached the end of the introduction and the beginning of the actual book. We hope these tips and ideas have helped, and that you can start getting ready for the actual lessons.

We wish you good luck in your Spanish studies, now and always…but above all, we hope you enjoy yourself!

Well, there's nothing left but to begin. Get ready!

CHAPTER 1

BASIC SPANISH LESSON

While we may have laid down the rules and led you into the book with the introduction, every teacher must start their class slowly, unless they wish to risk their students losing interest.

This chapter of the most basic lessons, aptly named *Basic Spanish,* will open the first doors for you in your learning and provide you a collection of tools for the most simple of conversations and circumstances you'll inevitably face.

Think of the three simplest situations you can encounter when talking with someone — whether in a foreign tongue or your own — what comes to mind first? The first will obviously be greetings, which is basically meeting them and exchanging your first words to each other. The second, which is less obvious, is when you need to make a request or a give a command for them to do something for you. This will be extra important in the healthcare field, considering that the assistance you are requesting may be of an urgent nature. The third, following the other two, is a farewell. This is just as important as a greeting, because you will need to show the correct measure of respect when addressing somebody.

Finally, you will be provided with a small lesson on basic grammar and how to use the fundamental tools of the language to communicate with other people. Pay attention to the pronunciation — you can make certain mistakes, but try to keep them at a minimum for now!

Greetings

While working in any field, regardless if it involves healthcare or not, you will certainly need to greet people and get to know them, at least briefly enough to get their names. In Spanish, greeting somebody and introducing yourself to them is mostly similar to English, but there are a few differences.

The most commonly-known greeting for English speakers when thinking of Spanish is *"Hola" (Oh-la),* which they say to any Spanish speaker they encounter. This is a common misconception — Spanish speakers only use *"Hola"* in an informal **"Hi"** manner, and you would be making somewhat of a mistake to address your boss with one, or somebody you don't really have a trustworthy relationship with.

The correct manner to address someone in the professional field is by referring to the time of day, as follows:

Buenos (Buey-nose) / Buenas (Buey-nas) + Time of day

In which **Buenos** is a masculine plural version of *"Good"* and **Buenas** is the feminine plural version. The time of day can be represented as *morning, afternoon* and *evening,* where the phrases **Buenos días (dee-az), Buenas tardes (tar-dez)** and **Buenas noches (no-ches)** represent each of the aforementioned, respectively.

Note how morning is a masculine noun preceded by a masculine *"Good"* **(Buenos),** and both afternoon and evening are preceded by the feminine *"Good"* **(Buenas).**

But that may not be easy to understand, so let's give you an example of each introduction:

- **Buenos días, señor (seh-nior).** = Good morning, sir.
- **Buenas tardes, gerente (heh-ren-teh).** = Good afternoon, manager.
- **Buenas noches, enfermera (en-fer-meh-ra).** = Good evening, nurse (female).

It's that easy. Of course, you may want to ask them how they are feeling, or what they are doing.

Examples:

- **Buenos días, señora (seh-niora), ¿cómo está?** = Good morning, madame, how are you?
- **Buenas noches, doctor (dok-tor), ¿qué hace (ah-se)?** = Good evening, doctor, what are you doing?

In this case, the expressions ***cómo está*** and ***qué hace*** mean *"how are you?"* and *"what are you doing?"* respectively, and are used to make the conversation a bit lighter. Be sure to use these prudently, however, since not everyone will be interested in answering these particular questions to you if you're not in their trust. Also, the accent (or *tilde)* situated over certain letters represents a stressed vowel, used for asking questions or defining which version of the word you're using. For example, *está* can be found as **ésta, está** and **esta;** this makes the use of *tildes* necessary to avoid confusion.

Introducing yourself is the logical next step in your conversation, of course, and it can be as easy as it is in English if you know the right way.

-   **Buenas tardes, mi nombre es...** = Good afternoon, my name is...

Though you can also use:

-   **Buenos días, me llamo (ya-mo)...** = Good morning, I am called...

These terms are interchangeable, and you will find that you can use both equally without having to worry about who you're talking to. When it comes to asking the question, however, the correct way is:

-   **¿Cómo te llamas (ya-mass)?** = What are you called?

Or

-   **¿Cuál es tu nombre?** = What is your name?

Now that we have completed our lesson on greetings in Spanish, it would be nice to move on. The next step will be to learn how to make a request or give a command.

Requests and Commands

It can be hard enough to ask for help or tell somebody to do something in your native language, but finding the correct way to do it in a tongue that you're learning can be a real nightmare. You wonder if you're being respectful enough, or if you're coming off as some kind of authoritarian. We know how tough it can be, which is why we've added a few examples of how to request or order something from somebody.

To make a request, you typically ask someone if they *can* do something, *please.* For example:

¿Puedes (pueh-des) venir, por favor? = Can you come, please?

Where *venir* means *come,* and also where you're trying to say this in the most respectful way possible. Additional examples include:

¿Podrías (poh-dree-as) llamar a tu padre, por favor? = Can you call your father, please?

On the other hand, commands are basically when you say:

Ven. = Come.

You are making a clear, simple command in this case. Other examples can include:

Dame eso. = Give me that.
¡Fuera de aquí (a-ki)! = Get out of here!
Tráelo (tra-e-loh). = Bring it/him.

The tone of the phrase also changes, with requests made in a softer voice than the sharp tone used for orders. You will typically find a better reaction to requests than orders, especially considering that many people feel intimidated by being talked to with authority. Learn to speak to people differently depending on how strong your relationship is, and you will find that more doors shall open for you.

Farewells

Talking of doors, you will eventually want to close the door and say goodbye to the people you've met. Goodbyes in Spanish can be just as straightforward as English in this case, with you as a student needing mainly to learn what kind of terms are used to say "See you later" to the person you've just talked to.

Here, you must be aware of how each term translates. Let's get to the examples so you can understand what we mean:

Hasta (az-tah) luego (lu-eh-go). = See you later.
¡Chao! = Bye!
Nos vemos pronto, doctor. = See you soon, doctor.
Adiós, amigo. = Goodbye, my friend.

Variations exist, with many of them involving the words, terms or manner of addressing the other person in the conversation, but the aforementioned examples are the four most common ways of saying farewell to somebody. Use them as you wish, making sure to use both *Chao* and *Adiós* accordingly (informally and formally, respectively).

Basic terms, tools and vocabulary

And so we reach the final section of our first lesson, and quite possibly one of the most important language lessons you will have received, ever. You see, for all the rules you may master and the phrases you may learn, you will always need a strong foundation to be able to communicate correctly.

In every language, this foundation represents the basic necessities that you will most commonly use day in, day out, and which will allow you to not only understand and express the simplest and most common terms in the language, but also act as building blocks for the rest of the vocabulary you will ever use.

Be aware that these are simple phrases, and that we will go more in-depth further into this book.

- **Basic terms and tools**

First of all, we must begin with the simplest of expressions — **Yo soy**, which means **I am** in English. But what if we need to talk about other people?

Tú eres = You are
Él es = He is
Ella es = She is
Nosotros somos = We are
Ellos son = They are

Note how these are easy to express and don't even need a pronunciation guide. Now, to say that you *have* something you must say **Yo tengo**. In the case of other pronouns, you must use:

Tú tienes (tieh-nez) = You have
Él tiene (tieh-neh) = He has
Ella tiene = She has
Nosotros tenemos (teh-neh-mos) = We have
Ellos tienen (tieh-nen) = They have

However, sometimes you might want to say that you *can*, and that will be expressed by saying **Yo puedo**. For other pronouns, you use:

Tú puedes (pueh-des) = You can
Él puede = He can

Ella puede = She can
Nosotros podemos = We can
Ellos pueden = They can

And for those times when you want to say you *can't?* Just add a "no" before **puedo, puedes, puede, pueden or podemos.** Now, there are other occasions where you'll want to tell someone that you *want* something. In that case:

Yo quiero (ki-e-ro) = I want
Tú quieres (ki-e-res) = You want
Él quiere (ki-e-re) = He wants
Ella quiere = She wants
Nosotros queremos (ke-re-mos) = We want
Ellos quieren (ki-e-ren) = They want

But if it's something you *need* and not something you want?

Yo necesito (neh-seh-si-to) = I need
Tú necesitas (neh-seh-si-tas) = You need
Él necesita (neh-seh-si-ta) = He needs
Ella necesita = She needs
Nosotros necesitamos (neh-seh-si-ta-mos) = We need
Ellos necesitan (neh-seh-si-tan) = They need

In a similar sense, you may need to add a demonstrative pronoun after these expressions. These are the words we know as "this", "that", "these" and "those". In Spanish, each noun has a gender, meaning we must add genders to these and many other words. This can make the process just a tiny bit more complicated, but you'll practice that as we move along each lesson. Let's take a look:

Este = This (neutral)
Esta = This (feminine)
Esto = This (masculine)
Ese = That (neutral)
Esa = That (feminine)
Eso = That (masculine)

Estos = These (neutral or masculine)
Estas = These (feminine)
Esos = Those (neutral or masculine)

Esas = Those (feminine)

Talking of "these" and "those", you may need to ask for "some", "a lot of" or "little" of something as a healthcare professional. To say these adverbs, you have to use the following:

Algo = Something
Un poco = Some
Bastante (bahs-tan-teh) = A lot
Poco = Little (amount)
Mucho = A lot of
Demasiado (de-mah-siah-do) = Too much/Excessive amount

Now, as healthcare professionals, the words "give" and "take" will regularly be used — you may ask a nurse to *give* a patient a medicine, or you may ask a patient to *take* something every eight hours. Let's start with *giving:*

Yo doy = I give
Tú das = You give
Él da = He gives
Ella da = She gives
Nosotros damos = We give
Ellos dan = They give

In the case of "taking", we have the following:

Yo tomo = I take
Tú tomas = You take
Él toma = He takes
Ella toma = She takes
Nosotros tomamos = We take
Ellos toman = They take

You must also say **toma** if you want someone to **take.** Add **esto, eso, estos** or **esos** and you can begin making sentences. Finally, we must address the usage of "come" and "go", something you'll use heavily in the hospital environment.

To say "come", you must say **ven.** However, to say it in terms of "coming":

Yo vengo = I come
Tú vienes (vi-eh-ness) = You come

Él viene = He comes
Ella viene = She comes
Nosotros venimos (ve-nee-mos) = We come
Ellos vienen (vi-eh-nen) = They come

To say "go", you must say **ve.** To say it in terms of "going":

Yo voy = I go
Tú vas = You go
Él va = He goes
Ella va = She goes
Nosotros vamos = We go
Ellos van = They go

In a final note, we must stress that these are only the most *basic* of terms you will be using in your environment and in Spanish as a whole, but they will still allow you to form sentences and express your needs. Practice them and use them every time you must — they will become your most commonly-used expressions.

-     **Basic vocabulary**

As promised, the following is a list of the basic vocabulary that you will need to know before starting this book, and which you will have to practice regularly for when you encounter them in your daily activities. We've ensured that the most common terms are included to keep you from having to research, and have divided them in a way that will help with your memorization techniques.

Parts of the body

Cabeza = Head
Cráneo (krah-neo) = Skull
Cara = Face
Frente = Forehead
Ojos (oh-hoss) = Eyes
Nariz (na-riss) = Nose
Boca (bou-ka) = Mouth
Cachetes = Cheeks
Pómulos (poh-mull-os) = Cheekbones
Barbilla (bar-bie-ja) = Chin
Dientes (dee-en-tess) = Teeth

Cuello (ku-ey-yo) = Neck
Hombros (om-bross) = Shoulders
Espalda = Back
Pecho = Chest
Costillas (kos-ti-jass) = Ribs
Brazos (brah-zos) = Arms
Codos (ko-doss) = Elbows
Manos = Hands
Muñecas (mu-nie-cas) = Wrists
Dedos = Fingers
Uñas (u-nias) = Nails
Abdomen = Abdomen
Caderas (ka-deh-ras) = Hips
Piernas (pee-er-nas) = Legs
Muslos (muss-los) = Thighs
Rodillas (row-dee-jass) = Knees
Tobillos (tow-bee-joes) = Ankles
Pies (pee-es) = Feet

Parts and objects in a room

Puerta (poo-er-tah) = Door
Piso (pee-sow) = Floor
Techo = Ceiling
Pared (pah-red) = Wall
Silla (see-ja) = Chair
Mesa (meh-sa) = Table
Alfombra = Carpet

Parts of the house

Cocina (coh-see-na) = Kitchen
Jardín (har-deen) = Garden
Sala = Living room
Comedor = Dining room
Habitación (a-bee-ta-si-on) = Bedroom
Escaleras (es-ka-leh-ras) = Stairs
Entrada = Entrance
Salida = Exit

Family and friends

Padre = Father
Madre = Mother
Hijo (ee-hoh) = Son
Hija (ee-hah) = Daughter
Hermano (err-mah-no) = Brother
Hermana (err-mah-nah) = Sister
Primo = Cousin (masculine)
Prima = Cousin (feminine)
Tío = Uncle
Tía = Aunt
Abuelo = Grandfather
Abuela = Grandmother
Novio = Boyfriend
Novia = Girlfriend
Esposo = Husband
Esposa = Wife
Amigo = Friend (masculine)
Amiga = Friend (feminine)
Compañero (com-pah-nie-row) = Colleague
Conocido (ko-no-see-doh) = Acquaintance
Desconocido = Stranger

With all of this now taken care of, your first task is to begin practicing everything you've read and getting familiarized with these and other terms that you will make use of continuously during your upcoming lessons. Go easy on yourself and continue only when you're ready — there's plenty more to come for our healthcare professionals in the next chapters.

By the way, from the following chapter onward, you will be provided with a vocabulary list relevant to the conversational story you will read immediately after. Take a good look at it and learn what the terms mean before you go ahead with the actual lesson, and don't forget that there's a translation on the next page after the Spanish conversation.

Now, without further delay, see you in Lesson 2!

CHAPTER 2

GETTING TO KNOW THE PATIENT
UNA SEGUNDA OPORTUNIDAD — A SECOND OPPORTUNITY

Vocabulary List

- **¡Alguien que me ayude!** = Somebody help me!
- **¿Estás bien?** = Are you okay?
- **Cubierto de sangre** = Covered in blood
- **Accidente de automóvil** = Car accident
- **Costillas fracturadas** = Fractured ribs
- **Soy médico** = I'm a doctor
- **Solicito una ambulancia** = I request an ambulance
- **¿Qué sientes?** = What do you feel?
- **Pulmón** = Lung
- **Bajo los efectos del alcohol o alguna droga** = Under the effects of alcohol or any drug
- **Respirar con normalidad** = Breathe normally
- **Me duele respirar** = It hurts to breathe
- **Me estoy agotando** = I'm getting really weary
- **Uno de tus pulmones no está funcionando bien** = One of your lungs isn't functioning normally
- **Estoy sangrando** = I'm bleeding
- **Aguanta el dolor** = Endure the pain
- **consumir alcohol y conducir** = Consume alcohol and drive
- **Cirrosis hepática** = Cirrhosis of the liver
- **Mareos** = Dizziness / Disorientation
- **Atendido** = Attended

Spanish

Fernando: ¡Auch! **¡Alguien que me ayude!**

Laura: ¿Qué sucede? **¿Estás bien? ¿Por qué estás cubierto de sangre?**

Fernando: No, no estoy nada bien. Pues porque tuve un **accidente de automóvil**, y siento que tengo las **costillas fracturadas**. Mi auto cayó allá abajo.

Laura: ¡Es cierto, que terrible! Pero hoy es tu día de suerte, y no sólo por salvarte de un accidente. **Soy médico** y te voy a ayudar. Por favor, descansa mientras solicito una ambulancia. **¿Qué sientes?**

Fernando: Puedo sentir algo afilado pinchando mi **pulmón**. De verdad creo que me fracturé.

Laura: ¿Sí? Voy a necesitar que te acuestes. ¿Hay alguien más contigo?

Fernando: No, sólo yo.

Laura: ¿Cómo te llamas?

Fernando: Me llamo Fernando, ¿y tú?

Laura: Soy Laura. ¿Y cómo sucedió el accidente?

Fernando: No lo sé, estaba conduciendo tranquilamente cuando mi auto se deslizó fuera de la carretera y se fue por ese barranco. Casi morí.

Laura: ¿Te encuentras **bajo los efectos del alcohol o alguna droga**?

Fernando: Pues, puede que sí tomé unos tragos de más, pero no pensé que sería tan grave.

Laura: Es bastante grave; has podido matar a alguien más. Tienes mucha suerte. ¿Puedes **respirar con normalidad**?

Fernando: **Me duele respirar**, y siento que **me estoy agotando**.

Laura: Eso puede ser que **uno de tus pulmones no está funcionando bien**. Relájate, que la ambulancia está en camino. ¿Es tu primera vez en un accidente de este tipo?

Fernando: Sí, pero espero que sea la última. **Estoy sangrando**, ¿crees que llegue al hospital con vida?

Laura: Por supuesto, sólo debes resistir un poco. **Aguanta el dolor**, tú puedes.

Fernando: Sí, tendré que hacerlo. Fue mi error por **consumir alcohol y conducir.**

Laura: No lo puedes volver a hacer. ¿Tienes hijos?

Fernando: Sí, dos. Un niño y una niña de cinco y tres, respectivamente.

Laura: Piensa en ellos para la próxima. Esto no debe repetirse.

Fernando: Sé que no, de verdad quisiera dejar el alcohol. Se me ha hecho difícil.

Laura: ¿Alguna vez te has intentado meter en grupo de ayuda para alcohólicos?

Fernando: No, pero debo intentarlo ahora.

Laura: ¿Sabes que el alcohol afecta el hígado? Podrías sufrir de **cirrosis hepática** más adelante en tu vida.

Fernando: Sí, doctora. De hecho, a veces no me siento bien. Tengo **mareos**, y mi memoria ya no es la misma. ¿Eso que viene ahí es la ambulancia?

Laura: Sí, pronto serás **atendido**. Espero que hayas aprendido tu lección y manejes prudentemente para la próxima, Fernando. La vida ha decidido darte una segunda oportunidad. Dudo que haya una tercera.

Fernando: Gracias Doctora Laura, tienes razón. Cometí un gran error pero haré las cosas bien esta vez.

Laura: Ven, déjame ayudarte a caminar. Todo estará bien pronto. Por cierto, dame tu número telefónico; quiero asegurarme de que cambiarás tu vida.

Fernando: Así será. Gracias doctora, estoy muy agradecido.

English

Fernando: Ouch! **Someone help me!**

Laura: What's wrong? **Are you okay? Why are you covered in blood?**

Fernando: No, I'm not okay at all. Because I've had a **car accident**, and I think I have **fractured my ribs**. My car fell down there.

Laura: I see, how terrible! But today is your lucky day, and not just because you've survived an accident. **I'm a doctor** and I'm going to help you. Please, have a rest while **I request an ambulance. What do you feel?**

Fernando: I can feel something sharp pinching my **lung**. I really think I've fractured them.

Laura: Yeah? I'm going to need you to lie down. Is there anyone with you?

Fernando: No, just me.

Laura: What is your name?

Fernando: My name is Fernando, and you?

Laura: I'm Laura. How did the accident happen?

Fernando: I don't know, I was driving calmly when my car slipped off the highway and fell down that cliff. I almost died.

Laura: Are you **under the effects of alcohol or any drug?**

Fernando: Well, I may have drunk a few more drinks than I should, but I didn't think it would be this serious.

Laura: It is quite serious; you could have killed somebody. You're very lucky. Can you **breathe normally?**

Fernando: It hurts to breathe, and I feel that **I'm getting really weary**.

Laura: That could mean that **one of your lungs isn't working as it should**. Relax, the ambulance is on its way. Is it your first time in an accident of this kind?

Fernando: Yes, but I hope it's the last. **I'm bleeding**; do you think I'll arrive at the hospital alive?

Laura: Of course, you just have to hold on for a bit longer. **Endure the pain**, you can do it.

Fernando: Yes, I'll have to. It was my own mistake for **consuming alcohol and driving**.

Laura: You can't do it again. Do you have children?

Fernando: Yes, two. A boy and a girl, of five and three, respectively.

Laura: Think about them next time. This cannot repeat itself.

Fernando: I know it can't, I've tried to quit drinking. It's been so difficult.

Laura: Have you ever tried joining a help group for alcoholics?

Fernando: No, but I must try now.

Laura: Did you know that alcohol affects your liver? You could suffer from **liver cirrhosis** further ahead in life?

Fernando: Yes, doctor. In fact, sometimes I don't feel well. **I get dizzy**, and my memory isn't what it used to be. Is that thing coming over there the ambulance?

Laura: Yes, you will be **attended** soon. I hope you learned your lesson and drive prudently next time, Fernando. Life has decided to gift you a second opportunity. I doubt there will be a third.

Fernando: Thank you, Doctor Laura. You're right. I made a huge mistake, but I'll do things right this time.

Laura: Come, let me help you walk. Everything will be okay soon. By the way, give me your phone number; I want to be sure you're going to turn things around.

Fernando: I will. Thank you, doctor, I'm very grateful.

CHAPTER 3

REQUESTING INFORMATION
LLAMADA AL 911 — 911 CALL

Vocabulary List

- **¿Cuál es su emergencia?** = What is your emergency?
- **No está nada bien** = Isn't in good shape
- **Se cayó** = He fell
- **Se dio un golpe muy fuerte** = Landed very badly
- **¿Cómo ocurrió el accidente?** = How did the accident take place?
- **Se resbaló** = He slipped
- **Impactando contra el suelo** = Slamming against the ground
- **No está muy lúcido** = He's not very lucid
- **Ha sufrido una caída grave** = He's has suffered from a serious fall.
- **¿Puede moverse?** = Can he move?
- **¿Puede hablar?** = Can he talk?
- **Sólo ligeramente** = Slightly
- **Recibió la mayor parte del daño** = Received the worst part of the damage
- **En su cabeza** = On his head
- **¿De cuántos pies fue la caída?** = How many feet did he fall?
- **¿Qué edad tiene su esposo?** = How old is your husband?
- **¿Sufre de la tensión?** = Does he suffer from blood pressure
- **Es un hombre sano y muy activo** = He's a healthy and very active man
- **¿Tiene alergia a algún medicamento?** = Is he allergic to any type of medication?

- **¿Aún se está moviendo?** = Is he still moving?
- **¿Le contesta sus preguntas?** = Does he answer your questions?
- **Acaba de responder a mi pregunta** = He just responded to my question
- **Trate de mantenerlo despierto** = Try to keep him awake

Spanish

Gonzalo: Sí, 911, **¿cuál es su emergencia?**

Stefania: ¡Mi esposo no está nada bien!

Gonzalo: Ok, señora; cuénteme, ¿qué le sucedió a su esposo?

Stefania: ¡Se cayó y **se dio un golpe muy fuerte!**

Gonzalo: De acuerdo, señora. **¿Cómo ocurrió el accidente?** ¿De dónde se cayó?

Stefania: Pues estaba haciendo un trabajo sobre el techo de la casa, pero al parecer **se resbaló** y cayó, impactando contra el suelo. **No está muy lúcido**, ¡y estoy muy asustada!

Gonzalo: De acuerdo, así que su esposo **ha sufrido una caída grave**. ¿Cuál es su ubicación?

Stefania: Estoy en Las Palmas, Calle 73, Casa 7. Es una casa azul.

Gonzalo: Perfecto, la ambulancia irá hacia allá en breve. Cuénteme, ¿su esposo **puede moverse? ¿Puede hablar?**

Stefania: Puede moverse **sólo ligeramente**. Ha hablado, ¡pero no parece saber qué le pasó o qué está sucediendo!

Gonzalo: ¿En qué parte del cuerpo **recibió la mayor parte del daño** por la caída?

Stefania: En su cabeza. Estoy muy preocupada, ¡creo que voy a llorar! ¡Debí estar ahí para él!

Gonzalo: Señora, por favor; no se culpe. Usted no hubiese podido detener su caída. **¿De cuántos pies fue la caída?**

Stefania: Aproximadamente de tres metros, o diez pies. Se resbaló y cayó bastante fuerte.

Gonzalo: ¿Qué edad tiene su esposo?

Stefania: Es un hombre de cuarenta y cinco años.

Gonzalo: Entiendo. ¿Cuál es su peso y estatura? **¿Sufre de la tensión?**

Stefania: No, **es un hombre sano y muy activo**. Pesa alrededor de ochenta kilogramos y mide un metro con ochenta.

Gonzalo: **¿Tiene alergia a algún medicamento?**

Stefania: No que yo sepa. Está muy mal, ¡necesitamos ayuda!

Gonzalo: Manténgase en línea, la ambulancia ya está a dos minutos de su ubicación. **¿Aún se está moviendo** su esposo? Si le habla, **¿le contesta sus preguntas?**

Stefania: Sí, aún se está moviendo. **Acaba de responder a mi pregunta.**

Gonzalo: Ok, **trate de mantenerlo despierto**. Necesitamos que se mantenga alerta para cuando la ambulancia llegue. ¿Puede hacerlo?

Stefania: Sí, señor. Intentaré.

Gonzalo: Ya debería estar llegando la ambulancia a su ubicación. ¿Puede verla?

Stefania: Sí, ¡ya la veo! ¡Muchas gracias!

Gonzalo: Tranquila, su esposo será atendido en seguida.

English

Gonzalo: Yes, 911, **what is your emergency?**

Stefania: My husband **isn't in good shape!**

Gonzalo: Ok, madam; tell me, what happened to your husband?

Stefania: He fell and **landed very badly**!

Gonzalo: All right, madam. **How did the accident occur?** Where did your husband fall from?

Stefania: Well, he was doing some work on the roof of our home, but apparently **he slipped** and fell, **slamming against the ground below. He's not very lucid** right now, and I'm very frightened!

Gonzalo: Okay, so it seems that your husband **has suffered from a serious fall**. What is your location?

Stefania: I'm on Las Palmas, 73 Street, house number 7. It's a blue house

Gonzalo: Perfect, the ambulance will be there shortly. Tell me, **can your husband move? Can he speak?**

Stefania: He can move, but only **slightly**. He's talked, but he doesn't seem to know what happened or what's going on!

Gonzalo: In what part of his body did he **receive the most damage** from the fall?

Stefania: On his head. I'm very worried; I think I'm going to cry! I should have been there for him!

Gonzalo: Madam, please; don't blame yourself. You wouldn't have been able to stop him from falling. **How many feet did he fall?**

Stefania: Approximately three meters, or ten feet. He slipped and fell considerably hard.

Gonzalo: How old is your husband?

Stefania: He's a forty-five-year-old man.

Gonzalo: Understood. **Does he suffer from blood pressure conditions?**

Stefania: No, **he's a very healthy and active man**.

Gonzalo: Is he allergic to any medication?

Stefania: Not that I know if. He looks really bad, we need help!

Gonzalo: Stay on the line, the ambulance is now only two minutes away from your location. **Is your husband still moving?** If he can talk, **can he answer your questions?**

Stefania: Yes, he's still moving. **He's just answered my question.**

Gonzalo: Ok, **try to keep him awake**. We need him alert for when the ambulance arrives. Can you do that?

Stefania: Yes, sir. I'll try.

Gonzalo: The ambulance should have reached you by now. Can you see it?

Stefania: Yes, I can see it! Thank you so much!

Gonzalo: Don't worry, your husband will be tended to right away.

CHAPTER 4

PEDIATRIC APPOINTMENT
UN DOLOR DE BARRIGA — A STOMACH ACHE

Vocabulary List

- **Pequeño** = Little one
- **Dolor de barriga** = Tummy ache
- **Dolor, diarrea y he vomitado dos veces** = Pain, diarrea, and I've vomited twice
- **Exámen de heces** = Stool exam
- **Altos niveles de parásitos** = High levels of parasites
- **Presencia de moco** = Presence of mucus
- **Señal de infección** = Signs of infection
- **Ecografía abdominal** = Abdominal ultrasound
- **Mujeres embarazadas** = Pregnant women
- **Infección estomacal** = Stomach infection
- **Medicamentos** = Medicines

Spanish

Christina: Buenas tardes, pase adelante. ¿Quién es el paciente?

Thomas: Yo, doctora.

Christina: Hola, **pequeño**. ¿Cómo te llamas? ¿Esta es tu mamá?

Thomas: Mi nombre es Thomas. Sí, pero mi mamá me dijo que hablara yo.

Christina: Perfecto, chico. Dime, ¿qué te trae a ti y a tú mami acá?

Thomas: Tengo un **dolor de barriga** desde hace dos días, y no me siento bien.

Christina: ¡Que mal! Cuéntame, ¿qué síntomas has tenido?

Thomas: ¿Síntomas? Pues, he tenido **dolor, diarrea y he vomitado dos veces**.

Christina: Entiendo. ¿Te hiciste un **examen de heces**?

Thomas: ¿De heces?

Christina: Sí, que si ya tomaste muestra de tu popó.

Thomas: Ah, sí. Acá mi mami tiene los resultados. Me los entregaron hoy.

Christina: Mmm, a ver. Estoy viendo que tienes **altos niveles de parásitos** en las heces. También tienes **presencia de moco**.

Thomas: ¿Moco? ¡Qué asco! ¿Qué puede significar eso?

Christina: Puede ser **señal de infección**, y eso puede que sea lo que está ocurriendo acá, el factor que te ha generado vómitos y diarrea.

Thomas: Está bien, doctora.

Christina: Por favor, quítate la camiseta y acuéstate aquí en esta cama. Necesito que te desabroches el pantalón también.

Thomas: De acuerdo, ya lo estoy haciendo. ¿Para qué me voy a acostar?

Christina: Quiero hacerte una **ecografía abdominal**, para poder dar un diagnóstico adecuado.

Thomas: ¡Vaya! Está bien.

Christina: Ahora, vas a sentir un poco de frío por este gel que te voy a esparcir sobre tu barriga. Tranquilo, es sólo para poder mirar mejor lo que ocurre adentro.

Thomas: ¿Es como lo que le hacen a las **mujeres embarazadas**, doctora? A mi mamá le hicieron eso para cuando nació mi hermanita.

Christina: Exacto, pero voy a ver qué te está haciendo ir mucho al baño. Relájate, voy a pasar este aparato por tu abdomen. Mmm… estoy viendo, y junto con los resultados de tu prueba, parece ser que tienes una **infección estomacal** causada por parásitos. Puedes taparte y volver a sentarte.

Thomas: Eso suena feo, ¿estaré bien?

Christina: Sí, amiguito, voy a necesitar que tu mami te compre estos siguientes **medicamentos**. Este es para el dolor, estos para la diarrea y el vómito, y este para proteger tu estómago. Las indicaciones están en el papel, síguelas al pie de la letra.

Thomas: Está bien, doctora. Voy a hacer todo lo que me dijo para curarme y sentirme mejor muy pronto. Gracias por todo. ¿Viste, mami? ¡La doctora dijo que me voy a sentir bien! ¡Adiós, doctora!

Christina: ¡Adiós, Thomas!

English

Christina: Good afternoon, come on in. Who is the patient?

Thomas: Me, doctor.

Christina: Hello, **little one**. What is your name? Is this your mom?

Thomas: My name is Thomas. Yes, but my mother told me to talk.

Christina: Perfect, son. Tell me; what brings you and your mommy here?

Thomas: I have had a **tummy ache** for two days, and I don't feel well.

Christina: That's terrible! Tell me, what symptoms have you had?

Thomas: Symptoms? Well, I've had **pain, diarrhea, and I've thrown up twice already**.

Christina: I understand. Did you do a **stool exam**?

Thomas: Stool?

Christina: Yes, I mean if you took a sample of your poop.

Thomas: Ah, yes. My mommy here has the results. I got them back today.

Christina: Mmm, let's see. I'm seeing **high levels of parasites** in your stool. You also have a **presence of mucus**.

Thomas: Mucus? That's gross! What could that mean?

Christina: It could be a **sign of infection**, and that could be what's going on here, the factor generating this vomiting and diarrhea.

Thomas: Okay then, doctor.

Christina: Please, take off your shirt and lie down on this bed. I also need you to unbutton your pants.

Thomas: All right, I'm doing it right now. Why am I lying down for?

Christina: I want to do an **abdominal ultrasound** on you, so that I can give you an adequate diagnostic.

Thomas: Wow! Okay.

Christina: Now, you're going to feel a little cold as I spread this gel over your tummy. Don't worry, it's just so that I can properly see what's going on in there.

Thomas: Is it like what they do to **pregnant women,** doctor? My mother got that done when she gave birth to my little sister.

Christina: Exactly, but in this case I'm going to see what's making you go to the toilet so often. Relax, I'm going to roll this tool over your abdomen. Mmm... I'm looking, and along with the results of your test, you seem to have a **stomach infection** caused by parasites. You can now cover yourself and sit down again.

Thomas: That sounds ugly, will I be okay?

Christina: Yes, buddy, but I'm going to need your mother to buy these **medicines**. This is for the pain, these are for your diarrhea and vomiting, and this one is to protect your stomach. The indications are on the paper, follow them to the letter.

Thomas: All right, doctor. I'm going to do everything you said so that I can cure myself and feel better soon. Thanks for everything. See, mommy? The doctor said I'm going to get better! Goodbye, doctor!

Christina: Goodbye, Thomas!

CHAPTER 5

ORDERING MEDICINE
FALLAS EN LA LOGÍSTICA — SUPPLY CHAIN FLAWS

Vocabulary List

- **El sistema** = The system
- **Nuestro servidor** = Our server
- **Trabajando a media máquina** = Working at mid-gear
- **Insumos** = Supplies
- **Cruciales para el funcionamiento del hospital** = Crucial to the functioning of the hospital
- **Reponer** = Replenish
- **Almacén** = Warehouse
- **Desabastecimiento** = Shortage
- **Rollos de gaza** = Rolls of gauze
- **Cinco docenas de cajas** = Five dozen boxes
- **Jeringas** = Syringes
- **Cargamentos** = Shipments
- **Sueros fisiológicos** = Saline solutions
- **Treinta cajas** = Thirty boxes
- **Tratamiento para quimioterapias** = Chemotherapy treatment
- **Agentes anestésicos** = Anesthetic agents
- **Cinco lotes** = Five batches
- **Antibióticos** = Antibiotics
- **Potabilidad de agua** = Water purification
- **Pastillas** = Pills

- **Fiebre** = Fever
- **Dolores musculares** = Muscular pain
- **Síntomas del Zika** = Zika symptoms
- **Enfermos de gripe** = Flu patients
- **Neumonía** = Pneumonia

Spanish

James: Estoy tan alegre de que estés acá, Michelle. No sé qué está sucediendo con **los pedidos**, que no están llegando al hospital.

Michelle: Sí, hay problemas en la **cadena de logística** de **la empresa**, James. Es algo que ver con **el sistema** en **nuestro servidor**, no está actualizando los registros, y eso nos tiene **trabajando a media máquina**.

James: Ya veo. Nos estamos quedando sin una serie de medicamentos e **insumos** que son **cruciales para el funcionamiento del hospital**. Independientemente de la razón, necesitamos **reponer** todo eso, ¿me entiendes?

Michelle: Sí, James. Entiendo completamente su necesidad. Por eso estoy acá.

James: Excelente, comencemos a caminar por el **almacén** entonces. Pronto entenderás por qué estoy tan preocupado.

Michelle: Vaya, ya veo. Está bastante vacío. Nunca lo he visto así. Hay un desabastecimiento grave entonces, ¿no?

James: No sólo grave. Gravísimo. ¿Estás tomando nota? Quiero comenzar a indicarte qué nos falta acá. Espero tengas papel y bolígrafo.

Michelle: Tengo mi teléfono inteligente, que es mejor.

James: Sí, bueno… estamos quedándonos sin **rollos de gasa**, para empezar, por lo cual voy a necesitar **cinco docenas de cajas**. ¿Me escuchaste bien? Cinco docenas.

Michelle: Sí, copiado. ¿Qué más?

James: Mis enfermeras se han estado quejando por la falta de **jeringas**. Ya sabes que de eso voy a necesitar **cargamentos**. Muchos cargamentos.

Michelle: ¿De cuánto estamos hablando?

James: Diez cargamentos de jeringas. Sí, bueno, ahora me gustaría comenzar con los medicamentos. ¿Tienes disponible **sueros fisiológicos**?

Michelle: Sí, de varios tipos.

James: Ya sabes, trae **treinta cajas** de sueros fisiológicos, además de la misma cantidad de tratamiento para quimioterapias que siempre me has suministrado. Ahora, para los **agentes anestésicos**...

Michelle: Tenemos estos, mira esta lista. Han llegado otros importados con tecnologías mejoradas.

James: Interesante. Tráeme **cinco lotes** de este, tres de este y cuatro de aquel. ¿Tienes **antibióticos**? Las infecciones deben tratarse, o sino vamos a tener noticias graves para los pacientes.

Michelle: Por supuesto. ¿Cuántas cajas quieres?

James: Envía un camión entero; hemos recibido muchos pacientes con infecciones estomacales y de colon por el problema de **potabilidad de agua**.

Michelle: ¿Necesitas acetaminofen? Hemos mejorado la fórmula para unas **pastillas** más efectivas. Sirven para dolores de cabeza, **fiebre**, **dolores musculares**, y ahora también para **síntomas del Zika**.

James: ¿Zika? Vamos a necesitar también de esas entonces. Bueno, lo demás que voy a pedir está en esta lista. Toma.

Michelle: A ver, a ver... Me parece que tenemos todo lo que buscas, me aseguraré de hacer llegar esta lista a mis superiores para que llegue el pedido tal como pediste.

James: Dame un tiempo estimado para recibir estos cargamentos; estamos urgidos con todo, y quiero que llegue a tiempo para no tener mayor escasez. Ya sabes que a esta fecha del año, comienzan a llegar los **enfermos de gripe** y **neumonía** por el frío.

Michelle: Por supuesto. Bueno, en veinte días te tendremos los primeros lotes en este mismo almacén. Cuenta con ello.

James: Perfecto. Debo dejarte, Michelle. Ya pasé mucho rato acá y tengo mis ocupaciones.

Michelle: De acuerdo, nos vemos en veinte días.

James: Sí, en veinte días. ¡Gracias de nuevo por venir!

English

James: I'm so happy that you're here, Michelle. I don't know what's going on with **the orders**, they're not reaching the hospital.

Michelle: Yes, there are problems with the **supply chain** at the moment, James. It has something to do with **the system** of **our server**: it's not updating our records, and it has made us **work at mid-gear.**

James: I see. We are running out of a series of **supplies** and medicines that are **crucial to the functioning of this hospital**. Regardless of why it's happening, we need to **replenish** them, do you understand?

Michelle: Yes, James. I understand your needs entirely. That is why I'm here.

James: Excellent, let's begin walking around the **warehouse**, then. You'll soon understand why I'm so worried.

Michelle: Wow, I can already see. It's very empty. I had never seen it like this. You're suffering from a bad **shortage**, no?

James: Not just bad. Seriously bad. Are you taking note? I want to begin to indicate what we're lacking here. I hope you have a pen and paper.

Michelle: I have my smartphone, which is better.

James: Yes, well... we're running out of **gauze rolls**, to start, which is why I'm going to need **five dozen boxes**. Did you hear me? Five dozen.

Michelle: Yes, copied. What else?

James: My nurses are complaining about a lack of **syringes**. You know that I'll need **shipments** of those. Many shipments.

Michelle: How many are we talking about?

James: Ten shipments of syringes. Yes, anyway, now I'd like to begin with medicine. Do you have **saline solutions**?

Michelle: Yes, of several kinds.

James: Well, you know, bring me **thirty boxes** of saline solutions, as well as the same amount of **chemotherapy treatment** that you've always supplied. Now, about the **anesthetic agents**...

36

Michelle: We have these, look at this list. A few new ones with improved technologies have been imported.

James: Interesting. Bring me **five batches** of these, three of these, and four of those. Do you have **antibiotics**? Infections must be treated, or we'll soon have to give bad news to our patients..

Michelle: Of course. How many boxes do you require?

James: Send a truckload; we've admitted many patients with stomach and colon infections due to the **water purification** problem.

Michelle: Do you need paracetamol? We've improved the formula for more effective **pills**. They work for headaches, **fevers**, **muscular pains**, and now even for **Zika symptoms**.

James: Zika? We're going to need some of those as well, then. Well, the rest I'm going to request is on this list. Here you go.

Michelle: Let's see, let's see... I believe we have everything you're looking for; I'll make sure my superiors receive this list so that you can receive everything just like you ordered.

James: Give me an estimate of time to receive these shiploads; we're running out of everything, and I want it to arrive on time to avoid a bigger shortage. You know that at this time of the year, the **flu and pneumonia patients** begin to arrive because of the cold.

Michelle: Of course. All right, in twenty days we'll have the first batches in this very same warehouse. Count on it.

James: Perfect. I have to leave you, Michelle. I've been here for too long, and I have to get back to my occupations.

Michelle: Very well, see you in twenty days.

James: Yes, twenty days. Thanks again for coming here!

CHAPTER 6

SURGERY

VIDA O MUERTE — LIFE OR DEATH

Vocabulary List

- **Doctor residente** = Resident doctor
- **Cirugía** = Surgery
- **Bastante joven** = Very young
- **Extirpación del tumor** = Tumor extirpation
- **Recopilaste** = Compiled
- **En observación** = Under observation
- **Exámenes de sangre, heces, orina** = Blood, stool, urine exams
- **Biopsias** = Biopsies
- **Monitorear** = Monitor
- **Estado de salud** = Health state
- **Aprendizajes** = Lessons
- **Carrera universitaria** = University degree
- **Quirófano** = Operating room
- **Anestesiado** = Anesthesized
- **Corte** = Cut (Noun)
- **Escalpelo** = scalpel
- **Apertura** = Opening (Noun)
- **Dos retractores** = Two retractors
- **Ecografía** = Ultrasound
- **Aguja de irrigación** = Irrigation needle
- **Sangrado** = Bleeding
- **Pinzas** = Forceps
- **Tejido** = Tissue

- **Tubería** = Tube
- **Pus** = Pus
- **Tijera** = Scissors
- **Bandeja** = Tray
- **Aguja para sutura** = Surgical suture needle
- **Suturar** = Suturing
- **Antiséptico** = Antiseptic
- **Esterilizado** = Sterilized
- **Me halagas** = You flatter me

Spanish

Maria: Hola y muy buenos días, ¿supongo que eres el **doctor residente** que me va a ayudar con la **cirugía** el día de hoy?

Jorge: Buenos días, ¡sí! Soy yo, el Doctor Jorge González. ¿Supongo que hablo con la Doctora María López?

Maria: Exactamente. Eres **bastante joven,** pero he oído cosas buenas de ti. ¿Qué piensas sobre la **extirpación del tumor** del paciente? ¿Ya **recopilaste** suficiente información?

Jorge: Sí, hemos tenido al paciente **en observación** por las últimas cuarenta y ocho horas. Le he hecho constantes **exámenes de sangre, heces, orina** y **biopsias** para **monitorear** su **estado de salud.**

Maria: Excelente. Mi última pregunta: ¿estás listo para esto? Será tu primera gran prueba, considerando todo lo que implica.

Jorge: Sí, estoy listo. Va a requerir todos los **aprendizajes** que obtuve durante mi **carrera universitaria**, además de toda la concentración del mundo, pero sí sé que todo saldrá bien.

Maria: Perfecto, entonces sígueme: vamos a subir al **quirófano.** Ya el paciente nos está esperando ahí.

Jorge: De acuerdo.

Maria: Aquí estamos, como verás, el paciente ya ha sido preparado. Acaba de ser **anestesiado** en este momento, así que vamos a comenzar. Por favor, voy a necesitar que realices el **corte.**

Jorge: Ya, déjame usar el **escalpelo.** Listo, ya abrí, doctora.

Maria: Ahora déjame abrir más esa **apertura.** Necesito **dos retractores,** por favor. Gracias, los pondré acá y acá para poder visualizar mejor el tumor. ¿Ya lo ves? Es grande, tal como lo vimos en la **ecografía.** No será tan fácil de sacar.

Jorge: Hay mucha sangre, déjame limpiar la herida con una **aguja de irrigación.** Acá le colocaré gaza para controlar ese **sangrado** y evitar la infección.

Maria: Excelente. Por favor, Doctor González, necesito unas **pinzas** para comenzar a separar el tumor del resto del **tejido**. ¿Puedes asegurar de mantener la herida abierta mientras hago eso?

Jorge: Sí, por supuesto. El paciente tiene un tumor de tamaño considerable, ¿no? Esto pudo haber sido evitado si hubiese venido a removerlo mucho antes.

Maria: Absolutamente cierto, ¿pero cómo educamos a las personas que creen tener siempre la razón? Ya estoy separando el tumor. Por favor, coloca una **tubería** aquí para succionar la sangre y el pus.

Jorge: Es mucha sangre, ya comienzo a succionar. Listo, están desapareciendo los fluidos. ¿Quieres la **tijera**?

Maria: Sí, es mejor. Una **bandeja**, por favor. Ya terminé el corte, y voy a sacar el tumor del cuerpo. También prepara la **aguja para sutura**. ¿Quieres hacerlo, o lo hago yo?

Jorge: Suturar es mi trabajo preferido. Déjamelo a mí.

Maria: Lo haces muy bien, continúa así. Voy a buscar más gasa para la herida, además del **antiséptico**. ¿Crees que puedes encargarte del resto una vez hayamos **esterilizado** y cerrado todo?

Jorge: Estoy seguro. De verdad fue de mucha ayuda tu presencia, doctora. No creo que pudiera haber hecho esto sin ti.

Maria: Sí hubieses podido, y pronto lo harás. Creo en tu capacidad. Tú puedes con esto y más.

Jorge: Me halagas, doctora. Muchas gracias.

Maria: De nada, Doctor González. Ahora debo irme. Espero estés bien. Suerte con el paciente.

Jorge: ¡Hasta luego!

English

Maria: Hello and very good morning, I guess you're the **resident doctor** that's going to help me out with the **surgery** today?

Jorge: Good morning, yes! It's me, Doctor Jorge Gonzalez. I suppose you're Doctor María Lopez?

Maria: Exactly. You're **very young**, but I have heard good things about you. What do you think about the **extirpation** of the patient's tumor? Did you **compile** enough information?

Jorge: Yes, we have had the patient **under observation** for the past forty-eight hours. I've done **constant blood, stool, urine and biopsy exams** on him to **monitor** his **health state**.

Maria: Excellent. My final question: are you ready for this? It will be your first great test, considering everything that it implies.

Jorge: Yes, I'm ready. It is going to require all of the **lessons** I learned during my **university degree**, as well as all of the concentration in the world, but I know that everything will end well.

Maria: Perfect, then follow me: we are going to go up to the **operating theatre**. The patient is awaiting us there.

Jorge: All right.

Maria: Here we are, as you can see, the patient has already been prepared. He has just been **put under anesthesia** in this precise moment, so we are going to begin. Please, I am going to need you to make the **cut**.

Jorge: Right, let me use the **scalpel**. Done, I've opened him up, doctor.

Maria: Now let me spread that opening even further. I need **two retractors**, please. Thanks, I'll place them here and here so that we can see the tumor more easily. Do you see it now? It's big, just as we saw on the **ultrasound** scan. It won't be that easy to remove.

Jorge: There is a lot of blood, let me clean the wound with an **irrigation needle**. Here I'll add gauze to control the **bleeding** and prevent infection.

Maria: Excellent. Please, Doctor Gonzalez, I need some **forceps** so that I can start separating the tumor from the rest of the **tissue**. Can you make sure to hold the wound open while I do that?

Jorge: Yes, of course. The patient has a tumor of a considerable size, right? This could have been avoided if he had come to get it removed earlier.

Maria: That's the absolute truth, but how do we educate those people who always think they're right? I'm separating the tumor from the rest of the tissue. Please, place a **tube** here so that it can suck in the blood and **pus**.

Jorge: It's a lot of blood; let me suck that right away. Done, the fluids are disappearing. Do you want the **scissors**?

Maria: Yes, it's best that way. A **tray**, please. I've finished the cut, and I want to remove the tumor from the body. Also, get a **surgical suture needle** for stitches. Do you want to do it, or should I?

Jorge: **Suturing** is my favorite task. Leave it to me.

Maria: You can do it quite well, continue that way. I'm going to look for more gauze for the wound, as well as the **antiseptic**. Do you think you can take charge of the rest once we've **sterilized** and sealed everything?

Jorge: I'm certain. Truly, your presence was of great help, doctor. I don't think I could have been able to pull this off without you.

Maria: You would have been able to, and you will. I believe in your capacities. You can do this and more.

Jorge: You flatter me, doctor. Thanks a lot.

Maria: You're welcome, Doctor Gonzalez. Now I must go. I hope you're well. Good luck with the patient.

Jorge: See you later!

CHAPTER 7

DELIVERING BAD NEWS
NO QUEDA MUCHO... —
NOT LONG LEFT...

Vocabulary List

- **Está pasando algo grave** = Something bad is happening
- **Las noticias no son tan buenas** = The news isn't so positive
- **No le han dado de alta** = Hasn't been released
- **No es muy sencillo** = Isn't that simple
- **Dirigiéndome** = On my way
- **Quejándose** = Complaining
- **Dolores en el estómago** = Stomach pains
- **He temido lo peor** = I've feared the worst
- **¿Por qué tanto misterio?** = Why so much mystery?
- **¿Hay algo que deba saber?** = Is there something I must know?
- **No va a ser fácil** = It won't be easy
- **Dime que no es cáncer!** = Tell me it's not cancer
- **Temo confirmar tus peores miedos** = I must confirm your worst fears
- **Tumor maligno** = Malignant tumor
- **Pared de su estómago** = Wall of her stomach
- **Un cancer bastante agresivo** = A very aggressive cancer
- **Salvar su vida** = Save her life
- **Ropa, toallas y otras prendas** = Clothes, towels and other garments
- **Esta noticia me partió el corazón** = This news broke my heart
- **¿Cuánto tiempo le queda?** = How long does she have left?

- **Pronósticos** = Forecast
- **Esparció a otros órganos** = Spread to other organs
- **Tratamientos de radiación y de quimioterapia** = Radiation treatment and chemotherapy
- **Prueba** = Test
- **Terrible castigo** = Terrible punishment
- **Maldición** = Curse
- **Factores genéticos** = Genetic factors
- **Chances de sobrevivir** = Survival chance
- **Diagnóstico** = Diagnostic
- **Apoyo incondicional** = Unconditional support

Spanish

Edwin: Doctora, ¡Espere! No se vaya aún, necesito hablar con usted sobre mi madre. Sé que **está pasando algo grave**, y que **las noticias no son tan buenas**. Ya son tres días desde que llegamos y **no la han dado de alta**.

Louise: Sí, joven. Entiendo tu preocupación. Bueno, lo de tu mamá **no es muy sencillo**. Voy **dirigiéndome** a mi oficina, si quieres me puedes seguir.

Edwin: Está bien. Ella tiene tiempo **quejándose** de los **dolores en el estómago**, y **he temido lo peor**. De verdad no quiero perder a mi madre; es lo único que tengo. La amo demasiado.

Louise: Nadie quiere perder a su madre. Vamos, ya casi llegamos a mi oficina. Ahí podremos hablar mejor.

Edwin: ¿Doctora? **¿Por qué tanto misterio? ¿Hay algo que deba saber?**

Louise: Bueno, ya estamos acá. Por favor toma asiento. **No va a ser fácil** escuchar lo que te diré.

Edwin: ¿Qué me estás tratando de decir? **¡Dime que no es cáncer!**

Louise: Edwin, **temo confirmar tus peores miedos:** tu madre tiene un **tumor maligno** en la **pared de su estómago**.

Edwin: ¡No puede ser! No puede ser... no puedo creerlo. Esto es demasiado para mí...

Louise: Es **un cáncer bastante agresivo**, por lo que ya comenzamos el tratamiento para poder **salvar su vida**. Voy a necesitar que traigas su **ropa, toallas y otras prendas** que la hagan sentir más en casa; tiene tres días acá, sí, pero ya no podremos dejarla ir por un tiempo.

Edwin: Esto es terrible, **esta noticia me partió el corazón**. Mi amada madre... ¿Cuánto tiempo la tendré conmigo? **¿Cuánto tiempo le queda?**

Louise: Aún no puedo decirte con precisión, pero los **pronósticos** no son muy agradables. Como ya dije, es agresivo. Tiene probabilidades de afectar otros órganos. Necesitamos luchar, eso sí.

Edwin: ¿Cuánto tiempo? Sólo dígame.

Louise: Si ya se **esparció a otros órganos**, entonces seis meses, aproximadamente.

Edwin: No... no puede ser cierto.

Louise: Levanta la cara, Edwin. Mírame. Tu madre puede salvarse aún, con **tratamientos de radiación y de quimioterapia**. Eso sí, todo dependerá de cómo la ayudemos con esta **prueba**.

Edwin: ¡No es una prueba! Esto es un **terrible castigo**, ¡una **maldición** que ella no merece! Mi madre no le hizo nada malo a nadie para que esto le haya pasado.

Louise: No podemos achacar la culpa a una maldición o un castigo; debemos entender que estas cosas pasan. Su padre murió también de cáncer, así como su hermano. Probablemente fue debido a los **factores genéticos**. No es momento de lamentarse.

Edwin: ¿Cómo que no es momento? ¡Me acabas de dar la peor noticia de mi vida! ¡¿Qué esperas?!

Louise: No es momento. Es momento de trabajar para salvarla, ¿o no? ¿Acaso ya te rendiste tan rápido?

Edwin: No, no me he rendido. Es sólo que... ¿cuántas personas sobreviven a algo así?

Louise: Si el cáncer no se ha expandido y podemos tratarlo antes de que lo haga, podemos aumentar sus **chances de sobrevivir** al menos cinco años más hasta un 67%. ¿No te suena bien?

Edwin: ¿En serio? Cinco años es más de lo que hubiese imaginado. ¿Crees que podamos tratarlo antes de que se expanda? Necesitamos hacerlo.

Louise: Sí, pienso que es posible. Pero necesito terminar de hacer mi **diagnóstico**. ¿Puedo contar contigo para que aprendas a ser lo más fuerte que has sido en toda tu vida? ¿Para que le des un **apoyo incondicional** a tu mamá?

Edwin: Sí... creo que tendré que hacerlo.

Louise: No tienes opción. Debes recordar que la víctima aquí es ella. Tú sólo debes ser fuerte. Olvídate del dolor que tú sufres. La única que importa es tu madre. Ahora dejemos de hablar de esto, y hablemos de lo que haremos.

Edwin: Sí, doctora, definitivamente. Tienes razón. Voy a ser fuerte. ¡Hablemos entonces!

Louise: ¡Así es!

English

Edwin: Doctor, wait! Don't leave yet, I need to talk to you about my mother. I know **something bad is happening**, and that the **news isn't so positive**. It has been three days since we arrived and she **hasn't been released**.

Louise: Yes, young man. I understand your worry. Well, your mother's issue **isn't that simple**. I'm **on my way** to my office; if you wish, you can follow me there.

Edwin: Okay. She has been **complaining** about the **stomach pains** for a while, and **I have feared the worst**. I really don't want to lose my mother; she is the only thing I have. I love her so much.

Louise: Nobody wants to lose their mother. Come on, we've almost made it to my office. We can talk even better there.

Edwin: Doctor? **Why so much mystery? Is there something I should know?**

Louise: Well, we've arrived. Please take a seat. **It won't be easy** to listen to what I have to say.

Edwin: What are you trying to tell me? **Tell me it's not cancer!**

Louise: Edwin, **I must confirm your worst fears**: your mother has a **malignant tumor** on the **wall of her stomach**.

Edwin: It cannot be! It cannot be... I can't believe it. This is too much for me...

Louise: It is a **very aggressive cancer**, which is why we've already begun the treatment to **save her life**. I'm going to need you to bring **clothes, towels and other garments** that will make her feel at home; she has been here for three days, yes, but we won't let her out for a long while.

Edwin: This is terrible, **the news broke my heart**. My beloved mother... How long do I have left at her side? **How long does she have left to live?**

Louise: I can't answer with precision right now, but the **forecast** isn't very positive. Like I said, the cancer is aggressive. It has a chance of affecting other organs. We need to fight, that's for sure.

Edwin: How long left? Just tell me.

Louise: If it has already **spread to other organs**, then six months, approximately.

Edwin: No... it cannot be true.

Louise: Lift your face up, Edwin. Look at me. Your mother can still be saved, with **radiation treatment and chemotherapy**. That said, it will all depend on how we help her with this great test.

Edwin: It's not a **test**! This is a **terrible punishment**, a **curse** that she doesn't deserve! My mother didn't do anything wrong to anybody for this to happen to her.

Louise: We can't lay the blame on a curse or a punishment; we must understand that these things happen. Her father died of cancer as well, as did her brother. It was probably due to **genetic factors**. It's not the time to feel sorry for ourselves.

Edwin: What do you mean it's not the time? You just gave me the worst news I've received in my life! What do you expect?!

Louise: It's not the time. It's time to work on saving her, or not? Have you already given up so quickly?

Edwin: No, I haven't given up. It's just that... how many people survive something like this?

Louise: If the cancer hasn't spread and we can treat it before it does, then we can increase her **survival chances** for at least five years more up to 67%. Does that sound good?

Edwin: Really? Five years is more than I would have imagined. Do you think we can treat it before it expands? We must do it.

Louise: Yes, I believe it is possible. But I need to finish making my **diagnostic**. Can I count on you to learn to be the strongest you've been in your life? For you to give **unconditional support** to your mother?

Edwin: Yes... I think I'll have to do it.

Louise: You don't have a choice. You must remember that the victim here is her. You only have to be strong. Forget about the pain you're suffering. The only person that matters is your mother. Now, let's stop talking about this and start talking of what we'll do.

Edwin: Yes, doctor, definitely. You're right. I'll be strong. Let's talk, then!

Louise: That's more like it!

CHAPTER 8

DIFFICULT PATIENT
UNIDAD DE QUEMADOS — BURN UNIT

Vocabulary List

- **Aplicar su tratamiento** = Apply your treatment
- **Me dolió bastante la última vez** = Hurt me a lot last time
- **No me interesa el tratamiento** = I don't care about the treatment
- **No van a curarse** = Won't heal
- **Quemaduras de segundo grado** = Second-degree burns
- **Brazo quemado** = Burned arm
- **Perder el miembro** = Lose your limb
- **Tomado a la ligera** = Taken lightly
- **Espantarnos** = Spook us
- **Aguantar el dolor** = Withstand the pain
- **Preste atención** = Pay attention
- **Levántese** = Get up
- **Recuperarme** = Recover
- **Obligarlo** = Force you
- **Agredirme** = Assault me
- **Te suspendan por maltrato** = Suspended for mistreatment
- **Pacientes incrédulos** = Stubborn patients
- **Amputada** = Amputated
- **No soportaba el dolor** = Couldn't stand the pain
- **Es demasiado** = It's too much
- **Gentil** = Gentle
- **Seré delicada** = I'll be gentle

- **Brazo herido** = Wounded arm
- **Parece una tortura** = This is like torture
- **Te debo las gracias** = I owe you a thank you
- **Lidiar** = Handle
- **Descanse** = Rest

Spanish

Jennifer: ¿Señor Alfredo Rojas? ¿Estás despierto? Necesito que se levante para **aplicar su tratamiento**.

Alfredo: No gracias, enfermera. **Eso me dolió bastante la última vez. No me interesa el tratamiento en este momento**; seguiré durmiendo.

Jennifer: Señor Alfredo, sus heridas **no van a curarse** si no se le aplica el tratamiento.

Alfredo: ¿Qué es lo peor que puede pasar? Ya tengo **quemaduras de segundo grado**, así que no creo que pueda empeorar.

Jennifer: Pues no creo que usted sepa, pero de no tratarse su **brazo quemado**, podría infectarse y eventualmente podría **perder el miembro**. No es algo para ser **tomado a la ligera**.

Alfredo: Ustedes todos dicen cosas así para **espantarnos**. Por favor vuelva después, que tengo mucho dolor.

Jennifer: Debe **aguantar el dolor** y colaborar. Es mi deber ayudarlo con esto, y no pienso irme hasta que me **preste atención**. Por favor, **levántese** que vamos a aplicar su tratamiento.

Alfredo: Lo siento. Voy a esperar que me den de alta para irme a casa y **recuperarme** allá. No me gusta este lugar.

Jennifer: Por favor, señor. Por última vez, le digo que tengo que aplicar su tratamiento. No me haga **obligarlo** a levantarse.

Alfredo: Ni se le ocurra **agredirme**, o voy a llamar al director del hospital. Puedo hacer que **te suspendan por maltrato**, ¡ya verás!

Jennifer: Nadie está siendo maltratado acá. ¡Colabore! ¿Usted acaso quiere perder el brazo? ¿Nunca ha visto una infección grave? Está bien, voy a traerle las fotos que tenemos para **pacientes incrédulos** como usted.

Alfredo: Perfecto, traiga lo que quiera. Sé que no me van a convencer.

Jennifer: Ya regresé. Mire acá. Mire como las personas pueden quedar de no tratarse las quemadas. Mira, esta persona tuvo que ser amputada. Esta otra **no soportaba el dolor**. Mire.

Alfredo: Oh, esto es demasiado... **Es demasiado**, de verdad. Bueno, está bien. Voy a colaborar, pero tienes que ser **gentil**. Me duele muchísimo.

Jennifer: Así está mejor. No se preocupe, que yo **seré delicada** con su **brazo herido**.

Alfredo: Eso espero. No me sirve de nada que empeores mi agonía.

Jennifer: Sólo resista si le duele; estoy haciendo algo bueno para su salud.

Alfredo: ¿Así que sí va a doler? ¡Ayyyyyyy! ¡Ya, ya, deténte!

Jennifer: Sólo resista, señor. No puedo hacer nada por el dolor. Debo usar esta crema o las cosas se pondrán peores.

Alfredo: Esto parece una tortura, ¡que alguien me ayude!

Jennifer: Ya terminé, ¿por qué sigue gritando?

Alfredo: Ah, bueno... Pensé que... Bueno, al final creo que no fue tan grave como pensé. Creo que **te debo las gracias**, y una disculpa. No debí resistirme tanto, pero fuiste bastante insistente.

Jennifer: Para eso estamos entrenadas las enfermeras: para saber **lidiar** con pacientes difíciles que no colaboran.

Alfredo: ¿Como yo?

Jennifer: Exactamente. Para pacientes como usted que piensa que queremos hacerles daño, cuando sólo queremos ayudarlos a que se curen. Me alegra de que se haya dado cuenta que era mi intención ayudarlo de un principio. Ahora, volveré a mi trabajo. **Descanse**.

English

Jennifer: Mister Alfredo Rojas? Are you awake? I need you to get up so that I can **apply your treatment**.

Alfredo: No thank you, nurse. That **hurt me a lot last time. I don't care about the treatment** at this time; I'll continue sleeping.

Jennifer: Mister Alfredo, your wounds **aren't going to heal** if you don't receive treatment.

Alfredo: What's the worst that can happen? I already have **second-degree burns**, so I doubt that it can get worse.

Jennifer: Well, I don't think you know this, but if your **burned arm** isn't treated, it could get infected and you could eventually **lose the limb**. It's not something to be **taken lightly**.

Alfredo: You all say things like that to **spook us**. Please come later, I'm in a lot of pain.

Jennifer: You have to **withstand the pain** and cooperate. It is my duty to help you with this, and I don't plan on leaving until you **pay attention** to me. Please **get up**, we're going to apply the treatment.

Alfredo: I'm sorry. I'm going to wait to be released so that I can go home and **recover** there. I don't like this place.

Jennifer: Please, sir. For the last time, I'm telling you I have to treat your arm. Don't make me **force you** to get up.

Alfredo: Don't even think of **assaulting me**, or I'll call the hospital's director. I can get you **suspended for mistreatment**, you'll see!

Jennifer: Nobody is mistreating anybody. Cooperate! Do you want to lose the arm, or what? Have you never seen a serious infection or what? Fine, I'm going to bring the photographs we have stored for **stubborn patients** like you.

Alfredo: Perfect, bring whatever you want. I know you're not going to convince me.

Jennifer: I'm back. Look at these. Look at how people can end up when their burns aren't treated. Look, these people had to undergo

amputation. This other one **couldn't stand the pain**. Look.

Alfredo: Oh, **this is too much**... Too much, for sure. Well, it's okay. I'm going to cooperate, but you have to be **gentle**. It hurts so much.

Jennifer: That's better. Don't worry, **I'll be gentle** with your **wounded arm**.

Alfredo: I hope so. It won't help at all if you worsen my agony.

Jennifer: Just resist if it hurts; I'm doing something positive for your health.

Alfredo: So it will hurt? Ahhhhhh! Stop, stop, enough!

Jennifer: Just resist, sir. I can't do anything for the pain. You must use this cream or things will get worse.

Alfredo: This is like torture, somebody help me!

Jennifer: I'm done, why are you still screaming?

Alfredo: Ah, well... I thought that... Well, in the end I think it wasn't as bad as I'd thought. I guess **I owe you a thank you**, and an apology. I shouldn't have resisted so much, but at the end you're very insistent.

Jennifer: That's what us nurses are trained for: to be able to **handle** difficult patients that don't cooperate.

Alfredo: Like me?

Jennifer: Exactly. Patients like you who think that we want to hurt them, when all we want to do is help them get better. I'm happy that you realized that my intention from the very beginning was to help you. Now, I'll get back to my work. **Rest**.

CHAPTER 9

KEEPING SOMEBODY AWAKE
ATROPELLADO — HIT BY A CAR

Vocabulary List

- **No siento mis piernas** = I can't feel my legs
- **¡No se intente parar!** = Don't try to get up!
- **Acaba de ser atropellado por un carro** = You just got hit by a car
- **La avenida** = The avenue
- **Sintiendo que pierdo la consciencia** = I can feel my consciousness slipping away
- **Va en una ambulancia** = You're in an ambulance
- **Golpe en la cabeza** = Blow to the head
- **Empeore su condición** = Worsen your situation
- **Muy peligrosos** = Very dangerous
- **Me duele todo el cuerpo** = My whole body hurts
- **Todo me da vueltas** = Everything is spinning around
- **Cierto apuro** = Bit of a rush
- **Necesitamos que aguantes** = We need you to hold on
- **Entrar en coma** = Fall into a coma
- **¿Es normal que no sienta mis piernas?** = Is it normal that I don't feel my legs?
- **Los dedos de mis pies** = My toes
- **Mis caderas** = My hips
- **¿Quedé inválido?** = Am I disabled now?
- **Aún estás recuperándote y asimilándolo todo** = You're still recovering and digesting everything
- **Lesión en la columna** = Spine injury

- **Desacomodó ciertas cosas** = It messed up some things
- **Toque humorístico** = Humorous touch
- **Todo está bajo control** = Everything is under control
- **Los médicos se van a encargar de aquí en adelante** = The doctors can take care from here on out
- **No acabe en una silla de ruedas** = Not end up in a wheelchair

Spanish

Steve: Oh mi Dios, **no siento mis piernas...** ¿Qué me pasó?

Felicia: Señor, ¡no se intente parar!

Steve: ¿Qué sucedió? ¿Quién está hablando? ¿Por qué estoy cubierto de sangre?

Felicia: Señor, **acaba de ser atropellado por un carro** mientras cruzaba **la avenida.**

Steve: ¡¿Qué?! ¡No puede ser! Con razón estoy **sintiendo que pierdo la consciencia.**

Felicia: Sí, señor. **Va en una ambulancia** hacia el hospital. Necesito que escuche mi voz, y que no se vaya a desvanecer. Ha sufrido un **golpe en la cabeza**, y no queremos que **empeore su condición**. Este tipo de accidentes son **muy peligrosos.**

Steve: Intentaré... pero no es fácil, me siento muy mal. **Me duele todo el cuerpo.** La cabeza más aún. **Todo me da vueltas.**

Felicia: Présteme atención, señor. Escuche mi voz y concéntrese. Ahora, ¿qué es lo último que recuerda?

Steve: Recuerdo que iba hacia el trabajo, con **cierto apuro** porque mi tren llegó tarde hoy. Compré un café y un croissant y fui hacia la avenida... ya no recuerdo más. No sé en qué momento me atropellaron. Me duele mucho, de verdad. ¿Voy a sobrevivir esto?

Felicia: Tenemos que llevarlo al hospital primero, pero tal parece que sí. ¿Cómo se llama? ¡Ey, no se duerma!

Steve: ¿Ah? Ah, sí. Me llamo Steve.

Felicia: De acuerdo, Steve. Estamos cerca, pero **necesitamos que aguantes**. El golpe fue fuerte, y podrías **entrar en coma**. ¿Entiendes que si entras en coma, todo cambia no?

Steve: Sí. Vaya. ¿Es normal que no sienta mis piernas?

Felicia: No. Cuéntame más sobre eso.

Steve: No puedo mover **los dedos de mis pies**, y no siento nada más allá de **mis caderas. ¿Quedé inválido?** ¿Por qué estoy tan relajado al respecto?

Felicia: Es el shock. **Aún estás recuperándote y asimilándolo todo.** Podrías tener una **lesión en la columna**, pero esperemos que no. Puede que haya sido simplemente el golpe en tu cabeza. **Desacomodó ciertas cosas.**

Steve: Así que mi esposa tiene razón en que estoy loco, ¿ahora sí? Ja, ja.

Felicia: Bueno, si deseas verlo con ese **toque humorístico** puede funcionar. Con tal de que estés despierto. ¿Cómo se llama tu esposa?

Steve: Alicia. Su nombre es Alicia, y...

Felicia. Vamos, despierta, Steve. ¡Steve! ¡Tienes que mantenerte despierto!

Steve: ¿Ah? Ah sí, su nombre es Alicia. Va a ser la primera en venir a verme, de seguro.

Felicia: Lo sé. De hecho, ya estamos llegando al hospital. Voy a llamarla desde tu celular para que le avises. Dile que **todo está bajo control**; no la vayas a asustar ni nada de eso.

Steve: Sí, de acuerdo. Gracias, en serio. Ok, listo, ya viene en camino. Suena más asustada que yo.

Felicia: Bueno, ya eso era todo lo que necesitábamos, estamos entrando al hospital. Creo que **los médicos se van a encargar de aquí en adelante**. ¿Crees que puedas resistir el resto del camino, o necesitas que te acompañe?

Steve: Descuida, creo que ya puedo lidiar con esto. Muchas gracias, espero que todo termine bien y **no acabe en una silla de ruedas**.

Felicia: Todo terminará bien; ¡suerte Steve!

English

Steve: Oh my God, **I can't feel my legs**... What happened to me?

Felicia: Sir, **don't try to get up!**

Steve: What happened? Who's talking? Why am I covered in blood?

Felicia: Sir, **you've just been hit by a car** while you were crossing **the avenue**.

Steve: What?! It can't be! No wonder **I can feel my consciousness slipping away**.

Felicia: Yes, sir. **You're in an ambulance** on the way to the hospital. I need you to listen to my voice, and avoid passing out. You've suffered **a blow to the head**, and we don't want **the situation to worsen**. This type of accident is **very dangerous**.

Steve: I'll try... but it isn't easy; I feel really bad. **My entire body hurts**. My head hurts even more. **Everything is spinning around**.

Felicia: Pay attention to me, sir. Listen to my voice and concentrate on it. Now, what is the last thing you remember?

Steve: I remember I was heading towards my job, in a **bit of a rush** because my train was delayed today. I bought a coffee and a croissant and walked towards the avenue... and I remember nothing else. I don't even know in what moment I was hit. It hurts a lot, to be honest. Am I going to survive this?

Felicia: We need to take you to the hospital first, but it seems that way. What is your name? Hey, don't fall asleep!

Steve: Ah? Ah, yes. My name is Steve.

Felicia: All right, Steve. We're close, but **we'll need you to hold on**. It was a strong blow, and you could **fall into a coma**. Do you understand that if you enter the coma, everything changes right?

Steve: Yeah. Wow. **Is it normal that I don't feel my legs?**

Felicia: No. Tell me more about that.

Steve: I can't move **my toes**, and I don't feel anything beyond **my hips**.

Am I disabled now? Why am I so relaxed about it?

Felicia: It's the shock. **You're still recovering and digesting everything**. You could have an **injury in your spine**, but we can hope not. It could simply be the blow to your head. **It messed up a few things**.

Steve: So my wife is right about me being nuts, at least now? Ha, ha.

Felicia: Well, if you wish to look at it with that **humorous touch**, then it can work. As long as you remain awake. What is your wife called?

Steve: Alicia. Her name is Alicia, and...

Felicia: Come on, wake up, Steve. Steve! You have to remain awake!

Steve: Ah? Ah yes, her name is Alicia. She'll be the first person to visit me at the hospital, for sure.

Felicia: I know she will. In fact, we're arriving at the hospital. I'm going to call her from your phone so that you can let her know. Tell her **everything is under control**; don't scare her or anything.

Steve: Yeah, of course. Thanks, seriously. Ok, done, she's on her way. She's more frightened than I am.

Felicia: Well that was all that we needed, we're entering the hospital. I think the **doctors can take care from here on out**. Do you think you can hold on for the rest of the way, or do you need me to accompany you?

Steve: Don't worry; I think I can handle this. Thanks a lot, I hope it all ends well and **I don't end up in a wheelchair**.

Felicia: It'll all end well; good luck, Steve!

CHAPTER 10

TEACHING A CLASS
ANATOMÍA — ANATOMY

Vocabulary List

- **Clase de anatomía** = Anatomy class
- **Cara nueva** = New face
- **Estudiante de cuarto semestre** = Fourth semester student
- **Me recomendaron ver esta materia con usted** = I was recommended to attend this class with you
- **Toma asiento y presta atención** = Take a seat and pay attention
- **Esqueleto** = Skeleton
- **Las partes del cuerpo** = The parts of the body
- **Hueso** = Bone
- **Brazo** = Arm
- **Codo** = Elbow
- **Mano** = Hand
- **Radio** = Radius
- **Todos nuestros deberes comunes** = All of our common tasks
- **Músculos** = Muscles
- **Pierna** = Leg
- **Rodilla** = Knee
- **Fíbula** = Fibula
- **Una caída** = A fall
- **No es tan frágil** = Isn't so fragile
- **Una patineta** = A skateboard
- **Saltando desde un segundo piso** = Jumping from a second floor
- **Cuello** = Neck

- **Cráneo** = Skull
- **Inclinar y girar la cabeza** = Bend and turn the head
- **Esternocleidomastoideo** = Sternocleidomastoid
- **Antebrazo** = Forearm
- **Supinador largo** = Supinator longus
- **Braquiorradial** = Brachioradialis
- **Examen oral** = Oral test
- **Gemelos** = Gastrocnemius
- **Músculo sóleo** = Soleus muscle
- **Tejido blando** = Soft tissue
- **Movilidad** = Mobility
- **¡Ligamento!** = Ligament!
- **Apéndice** = Appendix
- **Pregunta capciosa** = Trick question
- **Refugio de bacterias buenas** = Refuge for good bacteria
- **Intestino** = Intestine
- **Hasta el viernes** = See you on Friday

Spanish

Pedro: Buenos días, ¿esta es la **clase de anatomía** con la profesora Julia Álvarez?

Julia: En efecto. Bienvenido a mi clase, joven. Eres una **cara nueva**, no creo conocerte. ¿Cómo te llamas?

Pedro: Mi nombre es Pedro. Soy **estudiante de cuarto semestre**, y me **recomendaron ver esta materia con usted.**

Julia: Excelente, me gusta que hayas obedecido a la persona que te dio esa sugerencia. Bueno, **toma asiento y presta atención.** Parece que eres el único estudiante aquí.

Pedro: Sí, así parece.

Julia: Ahora, Pedro. ¿Ves este **esqueleto**? Vamos a repasar **las partes del cuerpo**. ¿Ya viste algo de esto en el semestre anterior?

Pedro: Sí, vi lo básico con el profesor Rojas. Ya tengo cierta idea de lo que vamos a ver acá.

Julia: De acuerdo. ¿Cómo se llama este **hueso**? Este que pasa por el **brazo**, conectando el **codo** con la **mano**.

Pedro: Ese hueso se llama el **radio**, profesora.

Julia: Excelente, Pedro. Es extremadamente importante para **todos nuestros deberes comunes**, y soportar los **músculos** que nos permiten agarrar cosas. ¿Y este hueso que pasa por detrás de la **pierna**, más debajo de la **rodilla**?

Pedro: Si no me equivoco, ese hueso tiene como nombre la **fíbula**. Es un hueso que alguna vez me fracturé en **una caída**.

Julia: ¿Cómo te caíste, Pedro? Ese hueso **no es tan frágil**, así que debes haber caído desde una gran distancia.

Pedro: Sí, profesora. Fue en **una patineta, saltando desde un segundo piso**. Fue una muy mala idea que nunca voy a repetir.

Julia: Terrible, ¿cómo pudiste hacer algo tan loco? Ahora vamos con los músculos. ¿Cómo se llama el músculo que sube desde el **cuello** hasta el **cráneo**, y que tiene bastante fuerza para permitirnos **inclinar y girar la**

cabeza?

Pedro: Sí, ya sé... tiene un nombre extraño... ¡Es el **esternocleidomastoideo**! Ese mismo es, ahora que lo recuerdo.

Julia: Exactamente ese es su nombre. ¿Y el que te pasa por el lado superior de tu **antebrazo**, permitiendo que lo dobles hacia arriba? ¿Tienes alguna idea de cómo se llama?

Pedro: Se llama **supinador largo**, aunque también es conocido como... **braquiorradial**. Así es que se llama.

Julia: Vaya, así que sabes bastante del tema. ¿Crees que podrías presentar un examen para verificar tus conocimientos y evaluarte adecuadamente? Puede que este curso tan básico de medicina no sea acorde a tu nivel.

Pedro: Sí, suena bien. Quiero presentar ese examen.

Julia: Será un **examen oral**, en el cual te haré preguntas parecidas a las anteriores pero con mayor nivel de dificultad. Tienes tres puntos por cada respuesta correcta y menos un punto por incorrecta. ¿Listo para comenzar?

Pedro: Sí. Creo que será fácil.

Julia: No te confíes. Perfecto, vamos con la primera: ¿qué músculo queda detrás de los **gemelos**? ¿Y qué función cumplen los gemelos?

Pedro: Los gemelos son parte de la pierna. Su mayor función es permitirnos impulsarnos cuando vamos a movernos. Y detrás de ellos, pues, está el **músculo sóleo**.

Julia: Excelente, tres puntos para ti. Próxima pregunta: ¿Cómo se llama el **tejido blando** que une los huesos y les da **movilidad**?

Pedro: Oh, ya va... Se llama algo así como... *¡Ligamento!*

Julia: ¡Bien! Tres puntos más, para un total de seis. Te falta una para pasar el examen con una nota perfecta.

Pedro: Excelente, estoy listo.

Julia: Última pregunta para culminar: ¿cuál es la función del **apéndice**?

Pedro: Oye, eso es trampa, ¡no estudié eso para la lección!

Julia: Vamos, Pedro. Tú sabes esto.

Pedro: Déjame ver, que no era parte del examen. La función del

apéndice era… Un momento, ¡el apéndice no sirve para nada!

Julia: Eso es incorrecto, Pedro, pero no te voy a quitar los puntos. Era una **pregunta capciosa**. Recientemente, los estudios demostraron que el apéndice funciona para como un **refugio de bacterias buenas**, las cuales serán liberadas si tu **intestino** se enferma gravemente.

Pedro: ¡Interesante, profesora! ¿Así que pasé?

Julia: Sí, ¡pasaste! Bueno Pedro, con esto culmina la clase de hoy. Nos vemos el viernes. Prepárate para otro examen sorpresa.

Pedro: De acuerdo. **Hasta el viernes**, profesora.

English

Pedro: Good morning, is this the **anatomy class** with Professor Julia Alvarez?

Julia: Yes, indeed. Welcome to my class, young man. You're a **new face**; I don't think I know you. What is your name?

Pedro: My name is Pedro. I'm a **fourth semester student**, and **I was recommended to attend this class** with you.

Julia: Excellent, I like that you obeyed the person that made that suggestion to you. Well, **take a seat and pay attention**. It looks like you're the only student here.

Pedro: Yes, it does seem that way.

Julia: Now, Pedro. Can you look at this **skeleton**? We're going to go over **the parts of the body**. Did you already see any of this in the previous semester?

Pedro: Yes, I saw the basics with Professor Rojas. I already have a certain idea of what we're going to learn here.

Julia: All right. What is this **bone** called? This one that runs through the **arm**, connecting the **elbow** with the **hand**.

Pedro: That bone is called the **radius**, professor.

Julia: Excellent, Pedro. It's extremely important for **all of our common tasks**, as well as supporting the **muscles** that allow us to grab things. And this bone that passes through the back of the **leg**, under the **knee**?

Pedro: If I'm not mistaken, that bone is called the **fibula** bone. It's a bone that I once fractured in **a fall**.

Julia: How did you fall, Pedro? That bone **isn't very fragile**, so you must have fallen from quite a tall height.

Pedro: Yes, professor. I was on **a skateboard, jumping from a second floor**. It was a very bad idea that I'll never repeat again.

Julia: Terrible, how could you do something so insane? Now we'll move to the muscles. What is the muscle that rises from the **neck** to the **skull**

called, which is strong enough to allow us to **bend and turn our head**?

Pedro: Yes, I know... It has a strange name... It's the **sternocleidomastoid**! That's the one, now that I remember.

Julia: That's exactly its name. And what of the one that can be found on the top half of your **forearm**, allowing you to bend it upwards? Do you have any idea what it's called?

Pedro: It is called the **supinator longus**, although it is also known as... **brachioradialis**. That's how it's called.

Julia: Wow, so you know a lot about the subject. Do you think you could take an exam so we can check your learning and evaluate you accordingly? This basic medical course may not be at your level.

Pedro: Yes, that sounds good. I want to take that exam.

Julia: It shall be an **oral test**, in which I will ask you similar questions to the previous ones but with an increased level of difficulty. You'll receive three points for each correct answer, and minus one point for each wrong answer. Ready to begin?

Pedro: Yes. I think it will be easy.

Julia: Don't get too confident. Perfect, let's start with the first: what muscle is found behind the **gastrocnemius**? And what is the actual role of the gastrocnemius?

Pedro: The gastrocnemius is part of the leg. Its most important function is to allow us to push ourselves forward when we're going to move. And behind it, well, is the **soleus muscle**.

Julia: Excellent, three points for you. Next question: What do you call the **soft tissue** that unites the bones and gives them mobility?

Pedro: Oh, wait a sec... It's called something like... ***Ligament!***

Julia: Great! Three more points, for a grand total of six. You need one more correct question to pass the exam with a perfect grade.

Pedro: Excellent, I'm ready.

Julia: Final question so we can finish: what is the role of the **appendix**?

Pedro: Hey, that's cheating; I didn't study that for the exam!

Julia: Come on, Pedro. You know this.

Pedro: Let's see, because this wasn't part of the exam. The role of the appendix was… Wait a minute, the appendix doesn't serve any functions!

Julia: That is incorrect, Pedro, but I'm not going to take any points away. It was a **trick question**. Recently, studies demonstrated that the appendix serves as a **refuge for good bacteria**, which will be released if your **intestine** suffers from a serious illness.

Pedro: Interesting, professor! So, did I pass?

Julia: Yes, you passed! Well, Pedro, we have now finished today's class. See you on Friday. Prepare yourself for another surprise test.

Pedro: All right. **See you on Friday**, professor.

CHAPTER 11

DISCUSSIONS WITH COLLEAGUES ACORDAR DISCREPAR — AGREE TO DISAGREE

Vocabulary List

- **Echado un ojo** = Taken a look at
- **Sala de emergencias** = Emergency ward
- **Diarrea** = Diarrhea
- **Dolores abdominales severos** = Severe abdominal pains
- **Síndrome de colon irritable** = Irritable bowel syndrome
- **Enfermedad crónica** = Chronic illness
- **Problemas digestivos** = Digestive problems
- **Lácteos** = Dairy products
- **Harina de trigo** = Wheat flour
- **Exceso de gases** = Excess gas
- **Agotamiento** = Weariness
- **Infección** = Infection
- **Parasitos** = Parasites
- **Condiciones salubres** = Sanitary conditions
- **Problemas de potabilización** = Water treatment problems
- **Intolerancia a la lactosa** = Lactose intolerance
- **Ciertos quesos** = Certain cheeses
- **Intolerantes** = The intolerant
- **Fatiga** = Fatigue
- **No dudo ni un momento** = I don't doubt it for a minute
- **Historial** = History

- **Menos actividad física** = Less physical activity
- **Difiero con usted** = I disagree
- **Medicamento antibiótico** = Antibiotic medicines
- **Salga perjudicada** = Being affected negatively
- **Discrepar** = Disagree

Spanish

Melanie: ¿Le has **echado un ojo** a los pacientes de la **sala de emergencias**, Philip? Había una en la cual yo estaba bastante interesada. Llegó sufriendo de **diarrea** y de **dolores abdominales severos**, y sus exámenes parecían indicar que sufre de algún tipo de **síndrome de colon irritable**.

Philip: Disculpa pero, ¿síndrome de colon irritable? Sí la visité y pasé tiempo revisando su caso, y no creo que la causa tenga que ver con algún tipo de **enfermedad crónica** como esa.

Melanie: ¿Ah no? ¿Por qué no? Cumple con los síntomas: tiene **problemas digestivos** cuando come **lácteos** y **harina de trigo**, no va regularmente al baño y tiene un **exceso de gases**. Incluso me ha hablado de sufrir de **agotamiento**. ¿Por qué no crees que sea colon irritable?

Philip: Sus exámenes hablaban de **infección** y **parásitos**, pienso que tiene más que ver con que no está comiendo comida preparada en **condiciones salubres**, y el agua que ha tomado tenía parásitos. Recuerda que en esta zona hay **problemas de potabilización**. Por cierto, creo que sufre más de **intolerancia a la lactosa** que del colon en sí.

Melanie: No estoy de acuerdo. Dijo que podía comer **ciertos quesos**, pero cuando se excedía sufría de gases. No que era imposible consumir este tipo de comidas.

Philip: Incluso los **intolerantes** pueden comer pocas cantidades de lácteos, eso no significa nada.

Melanie: ¿Cómo explicarías entonces la **fatiga** que sufre? Ya he tratado con pacientes con el síndrome de colon irritable, y esto se parece bastante a los más comunes. De hecho, **no dudo ni un momento** que esta joven sufra de esa enfermedad.

Philip: No, esto para mí no se parece. Fíjate, le encontré una alta cantidad de bacterias en sus resultados de la prueba de heces, y la paciente además parece haber estado sufriendo de los peores dolores últimamente. Si tuviera el síndrome, ya tendría un **historial** de síntomas.

Melanie: Pero también contó que ha tenido **menos actividad física** en el último año y ha comido más en la calle. Puede que su síndrome empeoró en este tiempo por estas mismas causas. Las razones están allí a la vista.

Philip: Difiero con usted, Doctora Melanie. Creo que deberíamos aplicar un **medicamento antibiótico** para evitar que se esparzan los microorganismos que la están afectando tanto. Le reduciré los lácteos también, y sería interesante ver cómo reacciona a una reducción de harina de trigo.

Melanie: No podemos aplicar antibióticos sin antes descartar el síndrome de colon irritable. Debemos asegurarnos de que no sea esta enfermedad antes de proseguir. Por supuesto, hay que curar la infección, pero no creo que sea la razón principal de sus dolores y problemas digestivos.

Philip: ¿Cómo quiere que arreglemos esto sin que la paciente **salga perjudicada** por nuestra discusión?

Melanie: Hagámosle una ecografía y podremos descartar o no la enfermedad, ¿le parece?

Philip: Tendríamos que cobrarle ese examen a la paciente.

Melanie: Yo misma lo pagaré. ¿Le parece? Pase lo que pase, vamos a acordar **discrepar**… pero igual tenemos que estar seguros de lo que está sufriendo.

Philip: Entendido. Bueno, eso haremos. Vamos a buscarla, es momento de saber lo que sucede acá.

English

Melanie: Have you **taken a look** at the patients in the **emergency ward** lately, Philip? There was one I was greatly interested in. She came in suffering from **diarrhea** and **severe abdominal pain,** and her tests seem to tell me that she has a type of **irritable bowel syndrome**.

Philip: I'm sorry but, irritable bowel syndrome? I did visit her and spent some time checking out her case, and I don't think that the actual cause has something to do with a **chronic illness** such as that one.

Melanie: Oh, no? Why not? She meets the criteria for the symptoms: she has **digestive problems** when she eats **dairy products** and **wheat flour,** she doesn't go regularly to the bathroom, and she has a lot of **excess gas**. She has even mentioned suffering from *weariness*. Why do you not think it's irritable bowel?

Philip: Her tests spoke of **infection** and **parasites;** I believe that her illness has more to do with the fact that she's not eating food prepared in **sanitary conditions,** and that she's been drinking water filled with parasites. Remember that in this area there are problems with **water treatment**. By the way, I think she's suffering more from a **lactose intolerance** than her actual colon itself.

Melanie: I don't agree. She said she can eat **certain cheeses,** but when she went too far she suffered from gases. Not that it was impossible to eat these types of foods.

Philip: Even the **intolerant** can eat small amounts of dairies, it doesn't mean anything.

Melanie: How then would you explain the **fatigue** she's suffering from? I've treated many patients with irritable bowel syndrome, and this is very similar to the most common of them. In fact, **I don't doubt for a minute** that this young woman suffers from that condition.

Philip: No, to me this isn't similar. Look, I found a large amount of bacteria in her stool exam results, and the patient also seems to have been suffering from the worst pains only recently. If she had the syndrome, she'd have a certain **history** of symptoms.

Melanie: But she also told me she has had **less physical activity** in the past year, and that she has eaten out more often. These precise reasons may have worsened her syndrome. The reasons are clear as day.

Philip: I differ, Doctor Melanie. I believe we should apply an antibiotic medication to avoid the microorganisms affecting her so much from spreading. I'll reduce her dairy intake as well, and it would be interesting to see how she reacts to a reduction of wheat flour.

Melanie: We cannot apply **antibiotic medicines** before ruling out the irritable bowel syndrome. We must make sure that it is not this particular illness before continuing. Of course, we must cure the infection, but I don't think it is the main reason behind her pain and digestive problems.

Philip: How do you want us to settle this without the patient **being affected negatively** by our argument?

Melanie: Let us test her with an abdominal ultrasound and be able to rule out the syndrome or not, is that okay?

Philip: We would have to charge the patient for that test.

Melanie: I will pay for it myself. What do you think? Whatever happens, let's agree to **disagree**... but we still must be sure what she's suffering from.

Philip: Understood. Well, we'll do that. Let's go and pick her up, it's time to find out what's happening here.

CHAPTER 12

OFFERING COUNSELING
UNA ETAPA DIFÍCIL — A TOUGH PERIOD

Vocabulary List

- **Todo ha estado un poco difícil últimamente** = Everything has been a little difficult lately
- **Estoy para escucharte** = I'm here to listen to you
- **Estoy deprimida** = I'm depressed
- **Tarea tediosa** = A tedious task
- **Estoy distante de mi familia** = Distant from my family
- **¿Cuánto tiempo has estado sintiéndote así?** = How long have you been feeling this way?
- **Sensación de vacío** = Feeling of emptiness
- **Desde que perdí a mi bebé** = Since I lost my baby
- **Trauma emocional** = Emotional trauma
- **Puede drenar a cualquier persona** = That could drain anybody
- **Fue algo tan repentino e inesperado** = It was something so sudden and unexpected
- **Era como si nada podía salir mal** = It was as if nothing could go wrong
- **Dolor muy fuerte en mi vientre** = Very strong pain in my belly
- **Una punzada** = Sharp pang
- **No se estaba desarrollando** = The baby wasn't developing correctly
- **Enfermedad congénita** = Congenital disease
- **No parecía estar tan afectado** = Didn't seem too affected

- **¿Es primera vez que vienes a un especialista?** = Is it the first time you've come to a specialist
- **Mi vida ha perdido sentido** = My life has lost meaning
- **Es posible que necesites medicación** = It may be possible that you require medication
- **Ocupar tu mente** = Occupy your mind
- **¿Cómo me recupero de este terrible dolor?** = How do I recover from this terrible pain
- **Terapia, paciencia y entendimiento** = Therapy, patience and understanding

Spanish

Fernando: Buenas tardes, Señorita Catherine, un placer tenerla acá. ¿A ver, qué la trae a mi consultorio?

Catherine: Buenas tardes, doctor. Bueno, no sé exactamente por dónde comenzar. **Todo ha estado un poco difícil últimamente**; incluso explicar lo que me sucede.

Fernando: Comienza por el principio. De todas maneras **estoy para escucharte**, así que no hay problema alguno de que me cuentes toda la historia con detalle.

Catherine: Está bien. **Estoy deprimida**: ya no quiero salir, ni estudiar para mis exámenes, incluso comer se me ha hecho como una **tarea tediosa**. Me alejé del hombre que alguna vez llamé mi novio, e incluso **estoy distante de mi familia**.

Fernando: De acuerdo, ¿**cuánto tiempo has estado sintiéndote así**?

Catherine: Tengo aproximadamente un mes con esta **sensación de vacío**… Es la misma cantidad de tiempo que ha pasado **desde que perdí a mi bebé**.

Fernando: Entiendo. Bueno, Catherine, la verdad es que sufriste de un **trauma emocional** bastante fuerte que **puede drenar a cualquier persona**. ¿Cómo fue que perdiste a tu bebé? Cuéntame de tu experiencia. **Tenemos que llegar a la raíz del problema.**

Catherine: Fue algo tan repentino e inesperado. Todo iba tan bien, y estaba tan feliz. **Era como si nada podía salir mal**, y todos nos preparábamos para recibir al pequeño Carlos. Una mañana, sentí un **dolor muy fuerte en mi vientre**. Era **una punzada** como ninguna otra que había sentido jamás, y en seguida supe que algo malo pasaba.

Fernando: Lo había perdido.

Catherine: Sí. El bebé **no se estaba desarrollando** bien dentro de mí, por una **enfermedad congénita**. Murió antes de que pudiera venir al mundo como tanto lo deseé. Murió, y se llevó mi vida con él.

Fernando: ¿Era el bebé de tu pareja?

Catherine: Sí, pero mi novio no parecía estar tan afectado. Por eso mismo lo dejé. No parecía importarle nada que perdimos a Carlos. Decía que podíamos tener otro, como si Carlos fuera una cosa y no una persona que quería nacer.

Fernando: ¿Es primera vez que vienes a un especialista para hablar de esto?

Catherine: Sí, y apenas eres la tercera persona que sabe sobre esto.

Fernando: Verás, Catherine, quiero que entiendas algo. No todos reaccionamos igual a los acontecimientos. Enfrentar esto sola no será nada fácil, y es injusto que saques de tu vida a tu pareja porque reaccionó de forma distinta a ti. De hecho, necesitas entender que quizás él está sufriendo de la misma manera pero sin compartirlo con nadie. Puede que a él le termine costando más regresar a una vida normal.

Catherine: ...Entiendo. Pero, ¿cómo debo hacer? **Mi vida ha perdido sentido**; ya no quiero ver a nadie ni salir a ninguna parte. Quiero estar en mi cama con las luces apagadas y el silencio arropándome.

Fernando: Es posible que necesites medicación, y bastantes distracciones para **ocupar tu mente** y que no sientas que tu vida no tiene sentido. Tiene bastante sentido, y tus seres queridos te aman más que a nada. El pequeño Carlos no quiere ser defraudado, así que debes vivir para él y con él.

Catherine: ¿Cómo hago eso si ya lo perdí para siempre?

Fernando: No lo has perdido, porque sólo basta con cargar una parte de él contigo el resto de tu vida para que siga con vida de alguna forma.

Catherine: ¿Una parte de él como qué?

Fernando: Como los recuerdos de las emociones que sentías cuando estaba cerca de nacer. De todas esas cosas que planeaste a su lado en tu mente. Y del amor que tenías guardado para él. Quiero que ese amor lo uses en tus seres queridos, y no los pierdas por algo así. No es sano para ti, ni siquiera.

Catherine: ¿Pero **cómo me recupero de este terrible dolor**, doctor?

Fernando: No es fácil, pero va a requerir de mucha **terapia, paciencia y entendimiento**. Sólo así podrás ver la vida como antes nuevamente.

¿Qué dices, comenzamos para que entiendas cómo te vas a mejorar?

Catherine: Me parece un buen plan, ¡comencemos!

English

Fernando: Good afternoon, Miss Catherine, a pleasure to have you here. Let's see, what brings you by my office?

Catherine: Good afternoon, doctor. Well, I'm not sure where exactly to begin. **Everything has been a little difficult lately**; even explaining what's going on with me.

Fernando: Start from the beginning. In any case **I'm here to listen to you**, so there's no problem if you tell me the whole story in detail.

Catherine: That's okay. **I'm depressed**: I no longer want to go out, nor study for my exams, and even eating has become a tedious task. I have distanced myself from the man I once called my boyfriend, and I'm even becoming **distant from my family**.

Fernando: All right, **how long have you been feeling this way?**

Catherine: Approximately a month has passed with this **feeling of emptiness**... It's the same amount of time that has passed **since I lost my baby**.

Fernando: I understand. Well, Catherine, the truth is that you suffered from an **emotional trauma** that was quite strong and **that could drain anybody**. How was it that you lost your baby? Tell me about your experience. We must reach the root of the problem.

Catherine: **It was something so sudden and unexpected**. It was all going so well, and I was so happy. **It was as if nothing could go wrong**, and we were all preparing ourselves to greet little Carlos to the world. One morning, I felt a **very strong pain in my belly**. It was a **sharp pang** like none I'd ever felt before, and I immediately knew that something was wrong.

Fernando: You had lost it.

Catherine: Yes. **The baby wasn't developing correctly** inside of me, because of a **congenital disease**. He died before he could come to this world as I desired so greatly. He died, and he took my life with him.

Fernando: Was he your partner's baby?

Catherine: Yes, but my boyfriend **didn't seem too affected**. That's exactly why I left him. He didn't seem to care at all that we lost Carlos. He said that we could have another, as if Carlos was just a thing and not a person that wanted to be born.

Fernando: Is it the first time you've come to a specialist to talk about this?

Catherine: Yes, and you're only the third person to find out about this.

Fernando: You see, Catherine, I want you to understand something. We don't all react the same way to events. Facing this alone will not be easy, and it is unfair that you push your partner out of your life because he reacted differently to you. In fact, you must understand that maybe he's suffering in the same way but without sharing it with anybody. Maybe it will end up being harder for him to return to a normal lifestyle.

Catherine: ...I see. But, what should I do? **My life has lost meaning**; I no longer want to see anyone or go anywhere. I want to be in my bed with the lights off and the silence wrapping itself around me.

Fernando: It may be possible that you require medication, and many distractions to **occupy your mind** and keep you from feeling that your life has lost meaning. It actually has a lot of meaning, and your loved ones love you more than anything. Little Carlos doesn't want to be disappointed, so you have to live with him and for him.

Catherine: How do I do it if I've lost him forever?

Fernando: You haven't lost him, because you only need to keep a part of him with you for the rest of your life for him to remain alive in some way.

Catherine: A part of him like what?

Fernando: Like the memories of the emotions you were feeling when he was about to be born. Of all those things that you planned at his side in your mind. And of the love you carried for him. I want you to use that love on your family and friends, and not to lose them because it happened. It's not healthy for you, nor anybody else.

Catherine: But **how do I recover from this terrible pain**, doctor?

Fernando: It isn't easy, but it will require a lot of **therapy, patience and understanding**. Only then will you manage to see life as you used to

84

once more. What do you think; do we begin so that you can understand how you're going to get better?

Catherine: It seems like an excellent plan, let's begin!

CHAPTER 13

DIFFICULT CONVERSATION
UNA RESPUESTA DECISIVA — A DECISIVE ANSWER

Vocabulary List

- **No tan bien, ¿pero qué más puedo decirte en mi situación actual?** = Not so well, but what else can I tell you in my current condition?
- **Hace que las cosas empeoren** = All it does is make things worse
- **Ha llegado el momento de que hablemos de algo importante** = I believe the moment has arrived for us to speak about something important
- **¿Qué tan grave es?** = How serious is it?
- **¿Cuánto tiempo le queda a la vieja Maude?** = How long has the old Maude got left?
- **El rendimiento que has tenido con el tratamiento de quimioterapia** = The performance you've had with the chemotherapy treatment
- **Debo decirte que el pronóstico es muy bueno** = I must tell you that the prognosis is very positive
- **El estimado inicial era de un año, pero eso ha incrementado** = The initial estimate was of one year, but that has increased.
- **Buena alimentación, un estilo de vida saludable y tratamiento al pie de la letra** = A good diet, a healthy lifestyle and if you can fulfill your treatment to the letter
- **Ya el cáncer se ha esparcido, y comenzarán a fallar tus órganos poco a poco** = The cancer has already spread, and your organs will gradually fail
- **Tu vida va a deteriorarse de manera drástica** = Your life is going

to deteriorate in a drastic manner

- **Lamentándolo mucho** = With great regret
- **¿O acaso debo resignarme a este destino?** = Or must I resign myself to this fate?
- **¿Cuáles son las opciones que me vas a plantear?** = What will be the options that you're going to offer me?
- **No puedo prolongar mi inevitable muerte** = I can no longer prolong my inevitable death
- **No es una decisión sencilla** = It isn't an easy decision
- **Nuestra medicina paliativa es la mejor del país** = Our palliative medicine is the best in the nation
- **Un esqueleto con vida** = A living skeleton

Spanish

Christopher: Buenas tardes, Sra. Parker. Estoy contento de que estés acá. ¿Cómo te has estado sintiendo?

Maude: Oh, doctor, ya sabes... **No tan bien, ¿pero qué más puedo decirte en mi situación actual?** Mi hermana se ha asegurado de que yo esté más o menos bien, y mi esposo no me permite ni barrer el piso ya.

Christopher: Eso suena genial, señora. Me alegra saber que estás recibiendo la ayuda que recomendé. No puedes estar trabajando duro, ya que sólo **hace que las cosas empeoren**.

Maude: De eso tengo certeza, pero estoy segura que también quisieran descansar. Recuerda que ambos también son personas mayores, y no es fácil.

Christopher: No, no lo es. Bueno, Maude — creo que **ha llegado el momento de que hablemos de algo importante**, y lo sabes. No es un tema fácil ni uno que querrías hablar en otras circunstancias, pero supongo que estás de alguna forma u otra preparada, ¿no?

Maude: ...Sí. Por supuesto. Ha llegado la hora, y lo sé. Vamos dime, **¿qué tan grave es? ¿Cuánto tiempo le queda a la vieja Maude?**

Christopher: De acuerdo. Bueno, estuve viendo tus resultados y **el rendimiento que has tenido con el tratamiento de quimioterapia**, además de las opiniones de mis colegas en el hospital. Para comenzar, **debo decirte que el pronóstico es muy bueno. El estimado inicial era de un año, pero eso ha incrementado.**

Maude: ¿Es en serio? ¿Incrementó? ¿Cuánto es ahora?

Christopher: Con **buena alimentación, un estilo de vida saludable y tratamiento al pie de la letra**, podrás vivir al menos otros tres años más, Maude.

Maude: ¿Tres? Bueno, es un alivio de cierta manera, aunque siento que hay malas noticias.

Christopher: Sí. Estos tres años no serán fáciles. El tratamiento podrá mantenerte viva, pero vas a sufrir de muchos dolores y tu cuerpo no volverá a ser el que es en estos momentos. **Ya el cáncer se ha esparcido, y comenzarán a fallar tus órganos poco a poco**. No podemos ocultarte esto, Maude; **tu vida va a deteriorarse de manera drástica.**

Maude: Lo supuse. ¿Así que no voy a morir, pero mi vida será un sufrimiento, no?

Christopher: Lamentándolo mucho, pues algo así.

Maude: ¿Entonces supongo que me vas a plantear unas opciones? Me imagino que tengo una decisión sobre lo que va a pasar ahora. **¿O acaso debo resignarme a este destino?**

Christopher: Sí, puedes escoger el camino que tomará tu vida. No quiero influir en tu decisión de ninguna manera, eso sí, pero espero que entiendas que ninguna de las dos posibles decisiones será fácil para ti o tus seres queridos.

Maude: Entiendo. Ahora, quisiera saber — **¿cuáles son las opciones que me vas a plantear?** ¿Seguro está entre morir ahora o vivir por tres años en agonía?

Christopher: No me agrada la manera como las expones, pero prácticamente es como lo dices. ¿Qué piensas al respecto? Puedo ayudarte durante estos tres años, buscando siempre los tratamientos que más te ayuden con tus problemas de salud y recomendándote cualquier método nuevo que salga para mantenerte viva.

Maude: Doctor Christopher, estoy muy agradecida de verdad; su trato ha sido excelente y ha demostrado un gran interés en ayudarme, pero creo que es momento de aceptar mi destino. **No puedo prolongar mi inevitable muerte**, por más que lo desee. Voy a decidirme por terminar las cosas ahora mismo.

Christopher: No es una decisión sencilla, pero francamente es la decisión valiente. ¿Está segura? De la misma forma, voy a asegurarme de que el final sea el menos doloroso posible. **Nuestra medicina paliativa es la mejor del país**, y podrá vivir feliz sus últimos meses.

Maude: Sí, eso espero. Esta es la mejor decisión para mí, para mi esposo y para mi hermana. Quiero que ellos me recuerden en mi mejor forma. Que no me recuerden como un casco de lo que alguna vez fui. **Un esqueleto con vida**. Prefiero que esto acabe mientras estoy sonriendo, ¿no cree usted?

Christopher: Respeto tu decisión. Debemos comenzar desde ya entonces. Estoy orgulloso de tí, Maude. No sé qué vendrá ahora, pero lo vamos a lograr juntos. Ya verás.

Maude: Así será. ¡Lo sé!

English

Christopher: Good afternoon, Mrs. Parker. I'm glad to see you here. How have you been feeling?

Maude: Oh, doctor, you know... **Not so well, but what else can I tell you in my current condition?** My sister has been making sure I'm more or less okay, and my husband doesn't even let me sweep the floor anymore.

Christopher: That's wonderful to hear, madam. I'm glad you're getting the help that I recommended. You can't be working hard, since **all it does is make things worse**.

Maude: I'm certain of that, but I'm sure that they need some rest as well. Remember that both of them are also elderly people, and it isn't that easy for them.

Christopher: No, it isn't easy at all. Well, Maude — **I believe the moment has arrived for us to speak about something important**, and you know it. It isn't an easy subject nor one that you'd want to talk about in other circumstances, but I guess that you're prepared in one way or another, right?

Maude: ...Yes. Of course. The time has come, and I know it. Come on tell me, **how serious is it? How long has the old Maude got left?**

Christopher: All right. Well, I was checking your results and **the performance you've had with the chemotherapy treatment**, as well as the opinions of my colleagues at the hospital. To start, **I must tell you that the prognosis is very positive. The initial estimate was of one year, but that has increased.**

Maude: Really? It increased? How much is it now?

Christopher: With **a good diet, a healthy lifestyle and if you can fulfill your treatment to the letter**, you could be looking at living for at least three years more, Maude.

Maude: Three? Well, it is a relief in a way, although I feel there are still bad news.

Christopher: Yes. Those three years won't be easy. The treatment might keep you alive, but you are going to suffer from many pains and your body won't ever be what it is right now at these moments. **The cancer has already spread, and your organs will gradually fail**, one after the other. We can't hide this from you, Maude; **your life is going to deteriorate in a drastic manner**.

Maude: I had guessed as much. So I'm not going to die, but my life will become a real suffering, right?

Christopher: With great regret, yes, something like that.

Maude: So then I suppose you're going to offer me some options? I guess I have a decision to make on what happens now. **Or must I resign myself to this fate?**

Christopher: Yes, you can choose the path that your life will take. I don't want to sway your decision in any way, just in case, but I hope you understand that none of the two possible decisions will be easy for you or for your loved ones.

Maude: I understand. Now, I would like to know — **what will be the options that you're going to offer me?** I guess that it'll be between dying now or living in agony for three years?

Christopher: I don't like the way you describe them, but it is practically as you are saying. What do you think about it? I can help you during these three years, seeking always the most helpful treatments that can handle your health issues, and recommending any new method that is released to keep you alive.

Maude: Doctor Christopher, I am very thankful indeed; your way of treating me has been excellent and you have shown a great interest in helping me, but I think it is time to accept my fate. **I can no longer prolong my inevitable death**, for all that I wish to. I'm going to decide to end things right now as they are.

Christopher: It isn't an easy decision, but frankly it is the brave one. Are you sure? In the same manner, I will make sure that your end is the least painful possible. **Our palliative medicine is the best in the nation**, and you will be able to live out your last months in happiness.

Maude: Yes, I hope so. This is the best decision for me, for my husband and for my sister. I want them to remember me in my best shape. Not for them to remember me as a shell of what I once was. **A living skeleton**. I would rather end this while I'm still smiling, don't you think?

Christopher: I respect your decision. We must start right away, in that case. I'm proud of you, Maude. I don't know what will come now, but we are going to accomplish it together. You'll see.

Maude: We will. I know it!

CHAPTER 14

LEGAL ADVICE
PROTEGIENDO UNA VÍCTIMA —
PROTECTING A VICTIM

Vocabulary List

- **Aún me siento atemorizado** = I still feel afraid

- **Tengo mucho miedo, creo que estoy en mucho peligro** = I'm very frightened; I think I'm in great danger

- **Puede ver los moretones en mi cara usted misma** = You can see the bruises on my face yourself

- **Estoy desesperado, ya esto debe parar** = I'm desperate, this has to stop

- **Tengo miedo de que algún día se pase de la raya y me mate** = I'm afraid that one day he'll take a step too far and kill me

- **Estoy preocupada por tu situación** = I'm worried about your situation

- **Traté de ocultarme** = I tried to hide

- **Me persiguió hasta mi habitación** = He chased me up to my bedroom

- **Me tiró contra la puerta** = He threw me against the door

- **Me dio un puñetazo en la cara** = Threw a punch into my face

- **Una patada me alcanzó en el hombro** = A kick slammed into my shoulder

- **Me defendí como pude** = I defended myself as I could

- **Me golpeó al menos cinco veces más** = He punched me at least five more times

- **Incluso perdí el conocimiento** = I even lost consciousness
- **Que quería que yo estuviera muerto** = That he wished I was dead
- **Quiero salir de ahí y no volver más** = I want to get out of there and never return
- **Nadie me va a ayudar** = Nobody is going to help me out
- **Hay más probabilidad de que mi papá me mate a golpes que la de recibir su ayuda** = There is a higher likelihood of my father beating me to death than receiving their help
- **Pues yo estoy aquí para ayudarte** = I'm here to help you
- **Tu papá no tiene derecho de agredirte físicamente así como lo hizo** = Your father has no right to physically harm you as he did
- **Puedes denunciarlo a la policía por esto** = You can report him to the police for this
- **Tenemos evidencias que podrían ponerlo tras las rejas** = We have evidence that could put him behind bars
- **Necesito que colabores para que lo llevemos ante la justicia** = I need you to cooperate if we're going to take him before a court of law
- **Estás protegido y amparado por la ley, y nadie te va a quitar eso** = You're protected and covered by the law, and nobody is going to take that away
- **Podemos formular una denuncia** = We could file a report
- **Organismo protector de los menores de edad** = Underage protective agency
- **Tu padre no puede salirse con la suya** = Your father can't get away with what he's doing

Spanish

Simon: Hola doctora, gracias por recibirme en su consultorio con tan poco aviso. **Aún me siento atemorizado.**

Margaret: No hay problema, Simon. Siéntate, sé que no te sientes nada bien y que requieres de mi ayuda en un momento tan delicado. ¿Quieres un café?

Simon: Sí, doctora. Pero más que un café necesito su ayuda. **Tengo mucho miedo, creo que estoy en mucho peligro.**

Margaret: Vamos, con calma, que voy a necesitar que me expliques bien el caso. Sólo así podré ayudarte, una vez me hayas proporcionado toda la información necesaria.

Simon: Claro, claro. **Puede ver los moretones en mi cara usted misma,** causados por mi padre en su ataque. **Estoy desesperado, ya esto debe parar.** Todos los fines de semana es lo mismo, hasta **tengo miedo de que algún día se pase de la raya y me mate.**

Margaret: Si es capaz de golpearte así, uno no puede saber hasta dónde puede llegar. **Estoy preocupada por tu situación,** pero juntos vamos a buscar una salida. Tómate tu café y comienza a contarme cuando estés más tranquilo.

Simon: Sí, claro. Bueno, ya casi... Ok, de acuerdo. Es momento de contar todo.

Margaret: Perfecto, adelante. Estoy anotando.

Simon: Mi padre llegó, como siempre, del bar a las seis de la tarde. Tenía desde el día anterior tomando alcohol, y mi mamá también estaba nerviosa cuando lo vio pasar por la puerta.

Margaret: De acuerdo... ¿qué pasó después?

Simon: Le pidió comida a mi mamá, quien fue directa a servirle. Pero luego comenzó a llamarme por mi nombre. Al principio **traté de ocultarme,** pero comenzó a gritar. No paraba de gritar mi nombre.

Margaret: ¿Y en ese momento tú saliste a atenderlo?

Simon: Sí, tuve que hacerlo. En ese preciso momento fui a ver qué quería, y él me miró con ira. Quería saber por qué había tardado tanto en responder a sus llamados. Me veía con una expresión de odio que ya había visto.

Margaret: ¿Qué hiciste en ese momento?

Simon: Le respondí que estaba haciendo mi tarea, y rápidamente me fui a mi habitación. Fue el peor error que pude cometer.

Margaret: ¿Por qué?

Simon: Me persiguió hasta mi habitación, gritándome y diciendo que le había dado la espalda. **Me tiró contra la puerta** y luego **me dio un puñetazo en la cara.** Traté de levantarme, pero **una patada me alcanzó en el hombro. Me defendí como pude,** pero **me golpeó al menos cinco veces más.** Por un momento **incluso perdí el conocimiento.**

Margaret: ¿Y tu madre? ¿Qué hacía mientras esto ocurría?

Simon: Le gritó que se detuviera. Al final él lo hizo, pero no sin antes insultarme.

Margaret: ¿Qué te dijo tu papá?

Simon: Que quería que yo estuviera muerto.

Margaret: Lo lamento mucho, Simon. Sé que te cuesta mucho asimilar esto, y te debes estar preguntando cuál es la salida para ti. No mereces vivir en esa casa más tiempo.

Simon: Es así. **Quiero salir de ahí y no volver más.** Aún así, no tengo mucho dinero, y **nadie me va a ayudar.** Mi única familia vive en el otro lado del país, y **hay más probabilidad de que mi papá me mate a golpes que la de recibir su ayuda.**

Margaret: Pues yo estoy aquí para ayudarte, y pienso que debes escuchar los consejos que te voy a dar. Primero, **tu papá no tiene derecho de agredirte físicamente así como lo hizo.** No por ser tu padre puede lastimarte de esa manera. De hecho, no por ser tu padre puede hacerte cualquier cosa que vaya en contra de tus deseos. **Puedes denunciarlo a la policía por esto.**

Simon: Sí, pero cuando vuelva estará más furioso y me hará más daño. También podría hacerle daño a mi madre.

Margaret: Tenemos evidencias que podrían ponerlo tras las rejas,

¿sabes? No se ve bonito el panorama para él si tu madre testifica en una corte. **Necesito que colabores para que lo llevemos ante la justicia.**

Simon: ¿Cómo quieres hacer esto? Estoy dispuesto a todo para salvar a mi mamá y a mí mismo.

Margaret: Verás, Simon... **estás protegido y amparado por la ley, y nadie te va a quitar eso. Podemos formular una denuncia** que no sólo irá dirigida a la policía, sino al **organismo protector de los menores de edad**. Esto va a requerir de tu colaboración, pero juntos podemos detener esto que está ocurriendo en tu hogar. **Tu padre no puede salirse con la suya.**

Simon: No. Ya es demasiado tiempo aguantando sus abusos. Necesitamos una solución. Quiero participar en esto.

Margaret: Perfecto. Si estás seguro, vamos a comenzar con la denuncia entonces. Aquí vamos, Simon. Pronto se acabará el sufrimiento tuyo y de tu madre.

Simon: No veo la hora de que sea así, doctora. ¡Mil gracias! Ahora, acabemos con esto de una buena vez.

English

Simon: Hello doctor, thanks for seeing me here in your office on such short notice. **I still feel afraid.**

Margaret: There's no problem with that, Simon. Sit down, I know that you're not feeling well at all and that you require my help in such a delicate moment. Do you want a coffee?

Simon: Yes, doctor. But more than a coffee, I need your help. **I'm very frightened; I think I'm in great danger.**

Margaret: Come on; keep calm, because I'm going to need you to explain the case well. Only then will I be able to help, once you've provided me with all of the necessary information.

Simon: Sure, of course. **You can see the bruises on my face yourself**, caused by my father in his attack. **I'm desperate, this has to stop.** Every weekend is the same; **I'm afraid that one day he'll take a step too far and kill me.**

Margaret: If he's capable of hitting you like that, then we can't be sure what his limits are. **I'm worried about your situation**, but together we're going to find a way out. Drink your coffee and start telling me once you feel more comfortable.

Simon: Yeah, sure. Well, almost done... All right now. It's time to spill the beans.

Margaret: Perfect, go ahead. I'm taking notes.

Simon: My father arrived, as always, from the bar at six in the afternoon. He'd been drinking alcohol since the day before, and my mother was also nervous when she saw him come in through the doorway.

Margaret: All right... what happened then?

Simon: He asked my mom for food, who went straight to serve him. But then he started calling me by name. At first **I tried to hide**, but then he started to shout. He didn't stop screaming my name.

Margaret: And in that moment you went out to meet him?

Simon: Yes, I had to. In that precise moment I went to find out what he wanted, and he looked at me with fury. He wanted to know why I had taken so long to respond to his calls. He looked at me with an expression of hatred that I had already seen before.

Margaret: What did you do at that moment?

Simon: I answered that I was doing my homework, and quickly made my way to my bedroom. It was the worst mistake I could have made.

Margaret: Why is that?

Simon: He chased me up to my bedroom, screaming at me and saying that I had turned my back on him. **He threw me against the door** and then **threw a punch into my face**. I tried to get up, but **a kick slammed into my shoulder. I defended myself as I could**, but **he punched me at least five more times**. For one moment, **I even lost consciousness**.

Margaret: And your mother? What did she do while all of this was taking place?

Simon: She screamed at him to stop. At the end he did, but not before insulting me.

Margaret: What did your dad say?

Simon: That he wished I was dead.

Margaret: I'm very sorry, Simon. I know it's hard for you to wrap your head around this, and you must be wondering what the way out is for you. You don't deserve to live in that house for much longer.

Simon: I know. **I want to get out of there and never return.** Even so, I don't have much money, and **nobody is going to help me out**. My only family lives on the other side of the country, and **there is a higher likelihood of my father beating me to death than receiving their help**.

Margaret: Well **I'm here to help you**, and I believe you should listen to the advice I'm going to give you. First, **your father has no right to physically harm you as he did**. Not because he's your father can he hurt you as he did. In fact, not because he's your father can he do anything to you that goes against your wishes. **You can report him to the police for this**.

Simon: Yes, but when he returns he will be even more furious and will hurt me. He could also harm my mother.

Margaret: We have evidence that could put him behind bars, you know? The picture doesn't look pretty for him if your mother testifies at court. **I need you to cooperate if we're going to take him before a court of law.**

Simon: How do you want to do this? I'm willing to do anything just to save my mother and myself.

Margaret: You see, Simon... **you're protected and covered by the law, and nobody is going to take that away**. **We could file a report** that not only would be directed to the police, but also to the **underage protective agency**. This will require your continued cooperation, but together we can stop what is taking place at your home. **Your father can't get away with what he's doing.**

Simon: No. It has been too long taking his abuse. We need a solution. I want to participate in this.

Margaret: Perfect. If you're sure, let's start with the report then. Here we go, Simon. Soon you and your mother's suffering will be over.

Simon: I really can't wait until it's like that, doctor. Thank you so much! Now, let's end this once and for all.

CHAPTER 15

PREGNANCY CONFIRMATION
LE TENGO BUENAS NOTICIAS — I'VE GOT GOOD NEWS FOR YOU

Vocabulary List

- **Revisar los resultados de mis pruebas** = Check the results of my tests
- **Problemas de nervios** = Nervous issues
- **Con mucha alegría y emoción** = With great joy and happiness
- **Embarazada** = Pregnant
- **Dos semanas de embarazo** = Two-week pregnancy
- **Problemas estomacales y vómitos** = Stomach problems and vomiting
- **Aumento de peso** = The weight gains
- **Dolores de cabeza** = Headaches
- **Pareja estable** = Stable partner
- **Me he protegido** = I've used protection
- **¡Soy estéril!** = I'm sterile!
- **Tiene que estar equivocado** = I really think you're mistaken
- **Biológicamente imposible** = Biologically impossible
- **Vas a ser mamá** = You're going to be a mother
- **Nivel de esterilidad** = Level of sterility
- **Tratamiento de fertilidad** = Fertility treatment
- **Jamás** = Never
- **Es un choque** = It's a shock
- **¿Deseas tenerlo, cierto?** = You do want to have it, right?
- **Madre soltera** = Single mother

- **Apoyarte financieramente** = Support you financially
- **Nadie me va a emplear así embarazada** = Nobody is going to employ me pregnant like this
- **¡Me van a matar!** = They're going to kill me!
- **Van a maltratarme e insultarme** = They'll mistreat me and insult me
- **Podrían botarme de la casa** = They could even kick me out of their home
- **Fundación protectora de las mujeres** = Women's protection foundation
- **Aconsejarme** = Advise me

Spanish

Sara: ¡Hola, doctor! Estoy de vuelta a la clínica tras cinco días, como usted me lo pidió. Me imagino que en este tiempo ha podido **revisar los resultados de mis pruebas** y **sacar conclusiones de lo que sea que me está sucediendo.**

Tim: De hecho, sí ha sido así. Ya he podido hacer un buen seguimiento de todos los resultados de tus exámenes. Tuvimos que ir bien a fondo para entender qué te estaba ocurriendo, pero ya tenemos una causa.

Sara: Cuénteme, entonces. La verdad que he estado muy preocupada, y este misterio no me ayuda con mis **problemas de nervios**. Casi no me he podido concentrar últimamente debido a ello.

Tim: **Con mucha alegría y emoción**, debo confirmarte que estás nada más y nada menos que **embarazada**, Sara. ¡Felicitaciones!

Sara: Ya va, ¡¿cómo?! Eso es imposible.

Tim: No, no lo es. Tienes **dos semanas de embarazo**, y por eso has tenido tantos **problemas estomacales y vómitos**. También se entiende más la razón por las que has presentado **aumento de peso**, y por qué los **dolores de cabeza**.

Sara: No creo que eso pueda ser. No he tenido **pareja estable** por un tiempo, **me he protegido** y además, doctor, ¡soy estéril! De verdad que **tiene que estar equivocado**, sin ofender. Estamos hablando de algo **biológicamente imposible**.

Tim: Sara, no es imposible. Es real, y está pasando ahora. Créeme cuando te digo que estás embarazada, y que **vas a ser mamá**. Entiendo que exámenes anteriores demostraron un **nivel de esterilidad**, pero puede que algo haya cambiado en tu cuerpo desde entonces. ¿Nunca has hecho **tratamiento de fertilidad**, cierto?

Sara: **Jamás**. En realidad ya nunca pensaba en tener un hijo. Esto... ¡no sé cómo reaccionar! Es decir, estoy feliz, ¡pero a la vez **es un choque** que no me permite ni siquiera pensar!

Tim: Así deberías sentirte. Jamás pensaste que tendrías un bebé, pero así será si lo deseas. **¿Deseas tenerlo, cierto?**

Sara: Sí, ¡definitivamente! Voy a tenerlo y amarlo muchísimo. Voy a cuidar a mi bebé y darle todo lo que necesite.

Tim: Excelente actitud. ¿Sabes quién es el papá? ¿Crees que puedas ponerte en contacto con él?

Sara: Sí, aunque es un chico con quien estuve saliendo apenas por un mes. No sé cómo lo tomará. ¿Y si no quiere aceptar el bebé? ¿Cómo podré sola con un niño o una niña? No me imagino siendo **madre soltera**.

Tim: Cálmate, Sara. Paso a paso. La ley protege a tu bebé y a ti, y lo obliga a **apoyarte financieramente**. Ya si decide **formar parte** de tu vida de nuevo queda de parte de él, pero no puedes depender de eso. Ahora se trata de tu bebé, independientemente de lo que pase.

Sara: Lo que pasa es que mis padres son los que me mantienen, y no tengo trabajo. **Nadie me va a emplear así embarazada**, y si les digo a mis padres que voy a tener hijo, **¡me van a matar!**

Tim: No creo eso. No creo que te matarían, después de estar tan preocupados por tu salud.

Sara: No los conoces, doctor. **Van a maltratarme e insultarme. Podrían botarme de la casa**.

Tim: Pues de ser así, deberás ir buscando un sitio para quedarte. ¿Tienes algún otro familiar o una amiga que pueda apoyarte? Y en cuanto a maltratos, puedes ir a la **fundación protectora de las mujeres** si algo pasa. No tienes por qué aguantar eso.

Sara: Bueno, bueno. Me ayuda mucho hablar con usted, doctor. ¿Puede **aconsejarme** sobre qué hacer ahora?

Tim: Sí. Como tu doctor, voy a dedicar tiempo para que veamos cuáles son los siguientes pasos. Todo poco a poco y con calma, pero saldrá bien al final. Ya verás.

Sara: Sí, eso pienso. Muchas gracias, doctor.

English

Sara: Hello, doctor! I'm back to the clinic after five days, just as you requested from me. I can guess that during this time you've been able to **check the results of my tests** and **reach conclusions of whatever it is that is happening to me**.

Tim: It has been that way, in fact. I've been able to do a **good analysis** of all the results of your exams. We had to **delve deep** to understand what was going on, but we have found a cause.

Sara: Tell me, then. The truth is that I have been very worried, and this mystery hasn't helped me with my **nervous issues**. I have **barely been able to concentrate lately** because of it.

Tim: With great joy and happiness, I must confirm that you are **pregnant**, Sara. Congratulations!

Sara: Wait, how?! That's impossible.

Tim: No, no it isn't. You have a **two-week pregnancy**, and that is why you've been suffering from so many **stomach problems and vomiting**. It's also easier to understand the cause behind **the weight gains**, and why you've had **headaches**.

Sara: I don't think that it can be the case. I haven't had a **stable partner** for a while, **I've used protection**, and also, doctor, **I'm sterile! I really think you're mistaken**, no offense. We're talking about something **biologically impossible** here.

Tim: Sara, it isn't impossible. It is real, and it is happening right now. Believe me when I say that you're pregnant, and that **you're going to be a mother**. I understand that previous tests demonstrated a **level of sterility**, but something may have changed in your body since then. You've never undergone any **fertility treatment**, right?

Sara: Never. In truth, I never thought I'd have a kid. This... I don't know how to react! I mean, I'm happy, but at the same time **it's a shock** that doesn't even let me think!

Tim: That's how you should be feeling. You never thought you'd have a baby, but it will be that way if you wish it. **You do want to have it, right?**

Sara: Yes, definitely! I'm going to have it and love it a lot. I'm going to take care of my baby and give it everything it needs.

Tim: Excellent outlook. Do you know who the dad is? Do you think you can make contact with him?

Sara: Yes, although he's just a guy I was going out with for barely a month. I don't know how he'll take it. What if he doesn't want to accept the baby? How will I manage on my own with a boy or girl? I can't imagine myself as a **single mother**.

Tim: Calm down, Sara. Step by step. The law protects you and your baby, and compels him to **support you financially**. Whether he decides to be a part of your life again or not depends entirely on him, but you can't count on that. Now it's about your baby, no matter what happens next.

Sara: The thing is that my parents are the ones supporting me, and I don't have a job. **Nobody is going to employ me pregnant like this**, and if I tell my parents that I'm going to have a baby, **they're going to kill me!**

Tim: I don't believe that. I doubt that they'd kill you, after being so worried about your health.

Sara: You don't know them, doctor. **They'll mistreat me and insult me. They could even kick me out of their home**.

Tim: Well in that case, you could start looking for a place to stay. Do you have another family member or a friend that can support you? And when it comes to mistreatment, you can go to the **women's protection foundation** if something happens. You don't have to endure any of that.

Sara: Okay, okay. It helps me a lot to speak with you, doctor. Can you **advise me** on what I should do now?

Tim: Yes. As your doctor, I'm going to dedicate some time so that we can see what your possible next steps are. Everything has to be step by step and with patience, but it will end well. You'll see.

Sara: Yes, I agree with you. Thanks a lot, doctor.

CHAPTER 16

CHILDBIRTH

¡YA VIENE EL BEBÉ! — THE BABY IS COMING!

Vocabulary List

- **¡Mi esposa está teniendo su bebé!** = My wife is having a baby!
- **Sí, soy enfermera** = Yes, I'm a nurse
- **¿Cuántos meses tiene su esposa?** = How many months into the pregnancy is she?
- **¿Para cuándo estaba pautada para dar a luz?** = When was she supposed to give birth?
- **Ya tiene ocho meses y medio** = She's eight and a half months in
- **Tenía que tener a nuestro bebé dentro de una semana** = She was supposed to have our baby within a week
- **¡Necesitamos ir a la sala de parto ya!** = We have to go to the delivery room as soon as possible!
- **Teníamos todo preparado para una semana y no hoy** = We had prepared ourselves for a week's time and not now
- **Por suerte, traje toda la ropa que ella va a necesitar una vez haya tenido al bebé** = Luckily, I brought all of the clothing she'll need once the baby has arrived
- **Agarre la mano de Alana y ayuda a calmarla** = Grab onto Alana's hand and help calm her down
- **Esto de ser madre no es cosa fácil** = This process of becoming a mother isn't easy work
- **¿Es su primer hijo?** = Is it your first child?
- **Vamos a necesitar que comience a respirar hondo y se tranquilice** = We're going to need her to start breathing deeply

and to calm down

- **Sí, es nuestro primer hijo** = Yes, it's our first child
- **El bebé ya está empezando a salir** = The baby is starting to come out
- **Comenzamos con el trabajo de parto ahora sí** = We've now truly begun the stage of labor
- **¿Ella debe pujar? Ya quiere que salga el niño** = Does she have to push? She wants him out right now
- **Debemos realizar un corte llamado episiotomía** = We must make a cut known as an episiotomy
- **Sólo es para ayudar a salir al bebé** = It's just to help deliver the baby
- **Le vamos a dormir la zona genital** = We're going to put her entire genital area to sleep
- **Ya tenemos el corte** = We've made the cut
- **Estamos haciendo la dilatación del cérvix para ayudar a salir el bebé** = We're dilating the cervix so that we can help the baby get out of there
- **Voy a necesitar que empujes, con un ritmo continuo** = I'm going to need you to push, with a continuous rhythm
- **¡El bebé ya está saliendo! ¡Puedo ver su cabeza!** = The baby is coming out! I can see its head!
- **¡Ya va a nacer tu pequeño!** = Your baby is about to be born!
- **Está luchando por salir** = He's fighting to get out
- **Tenemos que sacar su cabeza y hombro anterior primero** = We have to pull out his head and his anterior shoulder first
- **Luego será el posterior** = Then it will be the posterior
- **Sacaremos el resto de su cuerpecito** = We will extract the rest of his little body
- **¡Una última pujada!** = One last push
- **¡Nuestro hijo nació!** = Our boy has been born!
- **Mucha suerte con tu pequeño** = Good luck with your little boy
- **Voy a llamar a una compañera para que corte el cordón umbilical** = I'm going to call a fellow nurse so that she can cut

the umbilical cord

Spanish

Oscar: ¡Madre mía! ¡Que alguien nos atienda, por favor! Necesito una enfermera o un doctor, **¡mi esposa está teniendo su bebé!** ¿Hay algún médico que nos ayude?

Cecilia: Sí, soy enfermera. Dígame rápido, **¿cuántos meses tiene su esposa? ¿Para cuándo estaba pautada para dar a luz?**

Oscar: Pues **ya tiene ocho meses y medio,** se supone que **tenía que tener a nuestro bebé dentro de una semana.** No sé qué más puedo decirte, **¡sólo que necesitamos ir a la sala de parto ya!**

Cecilia: Excelente. ¡Asistente! ¡Venga, Juan, por favor! ¿Cómo se llaman usted y su esposa, señor?

Oscar: Soy Oscar, y ella es Alana. Todo esto ha sido una sorpresa, ya que **teníamos todo preparado para una semana y no hoy. Por suerte, traje toda la ropa que ella va a necesitar una vez haya tenido al bebé.**

Cecilia: Me parece muy bien. De acuerdo, el doctor ya viene. Vamos a levantar a Alana y acostarla en esta cama. Ten cuidado. Gracias por la ayuda, Juan. Ya puedes regresar a lo que estabas haciendo.

Oscar: El doctor ya llegó, que bueno. ¿Puedo quedarme acá ayudando de alguna forma?

Cecilia: Sí, agarre la mano de Alana y ayuda a calmarla. Lo va a necesitar. **Esto de ser madre no es cosa fácil.**

Oscar: De acuerdo. Aquí vamos.

Cecilia: ¿Es su primer hijo? Esto nunca es sencillo. **Vamos a necesitar que comience a respirar hondo y se tranquilice.**

Oscar: Sí, es nuestro primer hijo. Es una bendición para nosotros. Sí, ya estoy calmando a mi Alana. **Todo va a estar bien,** mi amor.

Cecilia: Ok, ya vamos a comenzar. Alana, sigue respirando así. **El bebé ya está empezando a salir.** ¿Qué necesita, doctor? De acuerdo, **comenzamos con el trabajo de parto ahora sí.**

Oscar: ¿Ella debe pujar? Ya quiere que salga el niño.

Cecilia: Ah, ¿es un varón? No, aún no. **Debemos realizar un corte llamado episiotomía**, pero esto no es nada serio. **Sólo es para ayudar a salir al bebé.** Dile a Alana que **le vamos a dormir la zona genital.**

Oscar: Está bien. Ella ha investigado mucho sobre eso, y tenía el presentimiento que así sería. ¿Ahora?

Cecilia: Bueno, **ya tenemos el corte**, y **estamos haciendo la dilatación del cérvix para ayudar a salir el bebé.** Tranquilo, todo está saliendo como queremos.

Oscar: Me siento peor que ella, creo. Estoy sudando; creo que me voy a desmayar.

Cecilia: ¡Nada de eso, Oscar! Te necesitamos despierto. Sé fuerte. Vamos, háblale. En dos minutos comenzaremos a sacar al bebé, así que tómate un respiro rápido y relájate.

Oscar: ¡¿Dos minutos?! Está bien, trataré de tranquilizarme.

Cecilia: Ya, pasaron los dos minutos. Vamos, Alana. **Voy a necesitar que pujes, con un ritmo continuo.** ¡Vamos!

Oscar: **¡El bebé ya está saliendo! ¡Puedo ver su cabeza!**

Cecilia: Exacto: por eso debes ayudar. ¡Tú puedes, Alana! Puja, puja, **¡Ya va a nacer tu pequeño!**

Oscar: Alana, tú puedes. Ya puedo verlo, **está luchando por salir.** Sé que no es fácil, pero ya está saliendo.

Cecilia: Ya casi, **tenemos que sacar su cabeza y hombro anterior primero. Luego será el posterior,** tras lo cual **sacaremos el resto de su cuerpecito.**

Oscar: Entendido. ¿Escuchaste, mi amor? Ya lo están haciendo.

Cecilia: Ya sacamos su hombro anterior. Ahora vamos con el hombro posterior.

Oscar: ¡Daniel ya viene en camino!

Cecilia: ¿Se llama Daniel? ¡Qué bonito nombre! Bueno, ya estamos sacando el cuerpo. Un poco de ayuda, doctor. De acuerdo, ya puedo sacarlo completo. **¡Una última pujada, Alana!**

Oscar: Ya está listo, salió, **¡nuestro hijo nació!** ¡Increíble, estoy impresionado! Muchas gracias doctor, y muchas gracias enfermera. Son unos ángeles. Ya nació mi pequeño Daniel.

Cecilia: Tranquilo, Oscar. **Mucha suerte con tu pequeño**. **Voy a llamar a una compañera para que corte el cordón umbilical** y se encargue del resto. Descansa, Alana, y suerte con todo.

English

Oscar: Mother of Mercy! Can someone tend to us, please! **I need a nurse or a doctor, my wife is having a baby!** We need a nurse or a doctor, my wife is giving birth! Is there any doctor available to help?

Cecilia: Yes, I'm a nurse. Tell me quickly, how many months into the pregnancy is she? **When was she supposed to give birth?**

Oscar: Well **she's eight and a half months in**, and **she was supposed to have our baby within a week.** I don't know what else I can tell you, except that **we have to go to the delivery room as soon as possible!**

Cecilia: Excellent. Assistant! Come, Juan, please! What are you and your wife's names, sir?

Oscar: I'm Oscar, and she is Alana. All of this has been a surprise, because **we had prepared ourselves for a week's time and not now. Luckily, I brought all of the clothing she'll need once the baby has arrived.**

Cecilia: That is quite smart. All right, the doctor is coming. We have to lift Alana and lay her down on this bed. Be careful. Thanks for the help, Juan. You can go back to what you were doing.

Oscar: The doctor's here, that's good. Can I stay here helping in any way?

Cecilia: Yes, **grab onto Alana's hand and help calm her down.** She's going to need it. **This process of becoming a mother isn't easy work.**

Oscar: All right. Here we go.

Cecilia: Is it your first child? This isn't ever simple. **We're going to need her to start breathing deeply and to calm down.**

Oscar: Yes, it's our first child. A blessing for us both. Yes, I'm calming my Alana right now. Everything is going to be okay, my love.

Cecilia: Ok, we're going to begin. Alana, continue breathing like that. **The baby is starting to come out.** What do you need, doctor? All right, **we've now truly begun the stage of labor.**

Oscar: Does she have to push? She wants him out right now.

Cecilia: Ah, so it's a boy? No, not yet. **We must make a cut known as an episiotomy,** but it won't be anything serious. **It's just to help deliver the baby.** Tell Alana that **we're going to put her entire genital area to sleep.**

Oscar: Okay. She's done a lot of research on that, and she had the feeling that it would be needed. What now?

Cecilia: Fine, **we've made the cut,** and now **we're dilating the cervix so that we can help the baby get out of there.** Don't worry; everything is turning out like we expected it to.

Oscar: I feel worse than her, I think. I'm sweating; I think I'm going to faint.

Cecilia: None of that now, Oscar! We need you awake. Be strong. Come on, talk to her. In two minutes we'll begin to deliver the baby, so take a quick breath and relax.

Oscar: Two minutes?! All right, I'll try to calm down.

Cecilia: Ok, the two minutes have passed. Come on, Alana. **I'm going to need you to push, with a continuous rhythm.** Go!

Oscar: **The baby is coming out! I can see its head!**

Cecilia: Exactly: that is why you have to help. You can do it, Alana. Push, push. **Your baby is about to be born!**

Oscar: Alana, you can do this. I can see him; **he's fighting to get out.** I know it's not easy, but he's almost out.

Cecilia: Almost there, **we have to pull out his head and his anterior shoulder first. Then it will be the posterior,** after which **we will extract the rest of his little body.**

Oscar: Understood. Did you hear, my love? They're doing it all right now.

Cecilia: His anterior shoulder is out. Now we're going with his posterior shoulder.

Oscar: Daniel is on his way!

Cecilia: His name is Daniel? What a beautiful name! Well, we're pulling his body out now. A bit of help, doctor. Okay, I can finally pull him out entirely. **One last push, Alana!**

Oscar: It's done, he's out, **our boy has been born!** Incredible, I'm amazed! Thank you so much, doctor, and thank you so much, nurse. You're both angels. My little Daniel has been born.

Cecilia: No problem, Oscar. **Good luck with your little boy. I'm going to call a fellow nurse so that she can cut the umbilical cord** and do the rest. Please rest, Alana, and good luck with everything.

CHAPTER 17

APPENDICITIS

NO ME SIENTO TAN BIEN —
I DON'T FEEL SO WELL

Vocabulary List

- **Me he sentido muy extraño en los últimos días** = I've been feeling really strange in the past days

- **No ha habido dolor de que hablar, pero no he tenido mucha hambre** = There hasn't been any pain to speak of, but I haven't had much hunger

- **Todo lo que he comido, me ha tocado vomitarlo** = Anything I have eaten, I've thrown up all over the place

- **¿Has tenido alguna fiebre?** = Have you had a fever?

- **¿Estás seguro que no has sufrido algún dolor?** = Are you sure there hasn't been any pain?

- **Realmente no me siento bien** = I really don't feel well

- **Me gustaría que me hicieras una revisión** = I would like you to perform a check-up on me

- **Quítate los zapatos y camiseta** = Take off your shoes and shirt

- **Comenzó desde la noche del sábado** = All of this began on Saturday night

- **Sensación incómoda** = Uncomfortable sensation

- **En seguida me volví a sentir bien** = I felt better right away

- **Comencé a sentirme mucho peor** = I began to feel much worse

- **Dime si te duele cuando te toco del lado izquierdo** = Tell me if it hurts when I touch you on the left side

- **Ahora, del lado derecho** = Now, on the right side
- **¿Te duele?** = Does it hurt?
- **Sí, eso dolió** = Yes, that did hurt
- **Sí, y tengo como náuseas** = Yes, and I feel nauseous
- **Siento inflamación y creo que sé por qué** = I feel the swelling and I believe I know why
- **Necesitas ser sometido a cirugía con urgencia** = You need to undergo an urgent surgery
- **Tenías un caso de apendicitis** = You had a case of appendicitis
- **Ya éste estalló y se convirtió en peritonitis** = It has since burst and become peritonitis
- **Esto se acaba de volver más peligroso** = This has just become much more dangerous
- **La apendicitis se presenta sin síntomas de dolor, y puede inflamarse silenciosamente** = Appendicitis can appear without any symptoms of pain, and it can swell silently
- **Sugerir seriamente que te operes hoy mismo** = I can't suggest anything other than you having an operation today
- **La peritonitis es la inflamación de la pared interna del abdomen causada por infección** = Peritonitis is an inflammation of the inner wall of your abdomen caused by infection
- **Esta condición podría costarte la vida** = This condition could cost you your life
- **Acepto entrar a cirugía** = I accept to go into surgery
- **¿Cuánto tiempo tardaré en recuperarme?** = How long will I take to recover?
- **Podrías tardar entre dos semanas a un mes tras unos días en observación acá en la clínica** = You could take between two weeks to a month after some days under observation here at the clinic
- **No puedes seguir haciendo ejercicios** = You can't continue

doing exercise

- **Vamos directo al quirófano. Prepara tus cosas.** = We're going straight to the surgery room. Prepare your things

Spanish

Dan: Hola Doctora Elisa, gracias por recibirme.

Elisa: No hay problemas, Dan. Toma asiento. ¿Qué sucede contigo, y por qué has venido el día de hoy?

Dan: Bueno, doc, **me he sentido muy extraño en los últimos días. No he sentido ningún dolor, pero no he tenido mucha hambre. Todo lo que he comido, me ha tocado vomitarlo.**

Elisa: Interesante, déjame tomar nota. **¿Has tenido alguna fiebre? ¿Estás seguro que no has sufrido algún dolor?**

Dan: No, pero **realmente no me siento bien. Me gustaría que me hicieras una revisión para** poder tomarme las medicinas que necesite.

Elisa: Vamos entonces, **quítate los zapatos y camiseta**, y acuéstate allí en esa camilla. Estaré contigo en un momento.

Dan: Excelente. Bueno, para agregar detalles: esto **comenzó desde la noche del sábado**, en la que estaba haciendo deporte. Tuve que parar y descansar por una **sensación incómoda**, pero **en seguida me volví a sentir bien.** No fue hasta hoy, martes, que comencé a sentirme mucho peor. Aparte de lo que le dije de los vómitos.

Elisa: De acuerdo, relájate y vamos a ver qué sucede. Respira, y **dime si te duele cuando te toco del lado izquierdo.**

Dan: No, doctora. Nada.

Elisa: Ahora, del lado derecho. ¿Te duele?

Dan: ¡Auch! **Sí, eso dolió. Sí, y tengo como náuseas.**

Elisa: Tengo un baño acá si necesitas vomitar, pero trata de resistir. **Siento inflamación y creo que sé por qué.** De nuevo, Dan.

Dan: Sí, me duele más de lo que pensaba. ¡Debo ir a su baño, me siento muy mal!

Elisa: Esperaré acá, entonces. No te preocupes.

Dan: Ya. Ya me siento un poco mejor. ¿Qué me sucede, doctora? Su cara me dice que ya tiene idea de lo que pasa.

Elisa: Pues sí, Dan. **Necesitas ser sometido a cirugía con urgencia —tenías un caso de apendicitis, pero ya éste estalló y se convirtió en peritonitis. Esto se acaba de volver más peligroso.**

Dan: ¡¿Qué?! ¡¿Estalló?! ¿Cómo paso eso si solo sentí dolor una vez? No puedo creerlo.

Elisa: A veces **la apendicitis se presenta sin síntomas de dolor, y puede inflamarse silenciosamente** hasta que sucede algo como lo que estamos viendo. Pero no puedo decirte más que **sugerir seriamente que te operes hoy mismo. La peritonitis es la inflamación de la pared interna del abdomen causada por infección. Esta condición podría costarte la vida**, por lo que hay que operar ya.

Dan: ¿Ya? **No estoy preparado para esto**. Mañana debo trabajar, y hoy...

Elisa: Si no estás preparado para perder la vida, entonces mejor es que te operes. **Te puedo hacer una constancia para que la entregues a tu jefe.** De verdad **no te tomes esto a la ligera.**

Dan: De acuerdo. **Acepto entrar a cirugía.** No quiero que esto empeore, pero jamás pensé que iba a salir de esta cita con una visita al quirófano. **¿Cuánto tiempo tardaré en recuperarme?**

Elisa: Eso dependerá de muchos factores, pero **podrías tardar entre dos semanas a un mes tras unos días en observación acá en la clínica. No puedes seguir haciendo ejercicios** por un par de meses mientras te curas.

Dan: ¿Sí? Eso es lamentable. Pero bueno, tendré que sacrificarme. Cuéntame, ¿qué viene ahora?

Elisa: Vamos directo al quirófano. Prepara tus cosas. Te necesito listo en una hora.

Dan: Excelente, lo haré. Gracias, doctora.

Elisa: Mejor dame las gracias cuando termine la operación.

English

Dan: Hello Doctor Elisa, thanks for seeing me.

Elisa: No worries, Dan. Take a seat. What's wrong with you, and what has brought you here today?

Dan: Well, doc, **I've been feeling really strange in the past days**. There hasn't been any pain to speak of, but I haven't had much hunger. **Anything I have eaten, I've thrown up all over the place.**

Elisa: Interesting, let me take note. **Have you had a fever? Are you sure there hasn't been any pain?**

Dan: No, but **I really don't feel well. I would like you to perform a check-up on me** so I can start taking the medicines that I need.

Elisa: Okay then, **take off your shoes and shirt**, and lay down on that bed. I'll be with you in a moment.

Dan: Excellent. Well, to add some details: **all of this began on Saturday night**, when I was exercising. I had to stop and rest because of an **uncomfortable sensation**, but **I felt better right away**. It wasn't until today, Tuesday, that **I started feeling worse**. As well as the vomiting that I told you about.

Elisa: All right, relax and let's see what happens now. Breathe, and **tell me if it hurts when I touch you on the left side.**

Dan: No, doctor. Nothing.

Elisa: Now, on the right side. Does it hurt?

Dan: Ouch! **Yes, that did hurt. Yes, and I feel nauseous.**

Elisa: I have a bathroom here if you need to throw up, but try to hold on. **I feel the swelling and I believe I know why**. Again, Dan.

Dan: Yes, it hurts more than I expected. I must go to the bathroom, I feel very bad!

Elisa: I'll wait here, then. Don't worry.

Dan: Done. Ok, I feel better. What is wrong with me, doctor? Your face is telling me that you have an idea of what's going on.

Elisa: Actually yes, Dan. **You need to undergo an urgent surgery — you had a case of appendicitis**, but **it has since burst and become peritonitis. This has just become much more dangerous**.

Dan: What?! It burst?! How did that happen if I only ever felt pain once? I can't believe it.

Elisa: Sometimes **appendicitis can appear without any symptoms of pain, and it can swell silently** until something like what we're seeing takes place. But **I can't suggest anything other than you having an operation today. Peritonitis is an inflammation of the inner wall of your abdomen caused by infection. This condition could cost you your life**, which is why we have to operate now.

Dan: Now? I'm not prepared for this. I have to work tomorrow, and today...

Elisa: If you're not prepared to lose your life, then the best thing to do is to get the operation done. I can help you with a record so that you can hand in to your boss. You really can't take this situation lightly.

Dan: Fine. **I accept to go into surgery**. I don't want this to get any worse, but I never thought I'd leave this appointment with a trip to the surgery room. **How long will I take to recover?**

Elisa: That will depend on many factors, but **you could take between two weeks to a month after some days under observation here at the clinic. You can't continue doing exercise** for a few months while you heal.

Dan: Yeah? That's unfortunate. But okay, I'll have to sacrifice it. Tell me, what's going to happen now?

Elisa: **We're going straight to the surgery room. Prepare your things.** I need you ready in one hour.

Dan: Excellent, I will. Thanks, doctor.

Elisa: I'd rather you thank me once the operation is done.

CHAPTER 18

NUTRITIONIST APPOINTMENT
VAS A TENER QUE BAJAR DE PESO — YOU ARE GOING TO NEED TO LOSE WEIGHT

Vocabulary List

- **Siento que estoy muy obesa** = I feel that I'm too obese

- **No puedo correr por largas distancias** = I can't run for long distances anymore

- **Todo el tiempo pienso en comer** = I think of eating all day

- **Eres nutricionista** = You're a nutritionist

- **No conozco tus hábitos de salud** = I don't know your health habits

- **¿Cuántas veces a la semana sales a hacer algún tipo de ejercicio o actividad continua?** = How many times a week do you go out to get some exercise or continuous physical activity?

- **Tres veces a la semana** = Three times a week

- **Necesitas sacar tiempo para ejercitarte y hacer al menos una hora de actividad fuerte diaria** = You need to make time to get exercise and spend at least one hour a day on strong activity

- **Me gustaría saber qué tipo de dieta necesitaría hacer para poder comenzar a perder estos kilos** = I would also like to know what kind of diet I need to do so that I can start losing these excess pounds

- **¿Comes muchos alimentos con harina de trigo?** = Do you eat many different foods made from wheat flour?

- **¿Consumes azúcares en altas cantidades?** = Do you eat large quantities of sugar?

- **¿Tienes un consumo moderado de alimentos fritos, y comida rápida?** = Do you have a moderate consumption of fried food and fast food?

- **Trato de no comer comida rápida, aunque tomo muchas bebidas carbonatadas** = I try not to eat fast food, although I drink many carbonated beverages

- **La harina de trigo no te está aportando los nutrientes** = Wheat flour isn't really giving you any nutrients

- **No estás alimentándote bien** = You're not nourishing yourself properly

- **Los azúcares no sólo llevan hasta un incremento de peso, sino que pueden traer problemas de azúcar en la sangre y una probabilidad más alta de sufrir del corazón** = Sugars don't just lead to an increase in weight, but they also can cause problems with sugar in the blood

- **Necesitas comenzar primero con eliminar los azúcares** = You need to start with getting rid of sugars

- **Trata de comer frutas** = Try to eat fruits

- **Vas a intentar comer menos calorías en cada comida** = You're going to try to eat less calories in each meal

- **Puedes comer cinco veces al día** = You can eat five times a day

- **Comidas ligeras** = Light meals

- **Con vegetales crudos** = With uncooked vegetables

- **Trata de cocinar tus alimentos a la plancha o hervirlos** = Try to cook your meals grilled or boiled

- **No utilices aceite ni grasa para cocinar** = Don't use oil or fat to cook

- **Trata de no comer cerdo. Tiene mucha grasa** = Try not to eat pork. It has a lot of fat

- **Cortes sin grasa** = Fatless cuts

- **Sólo podrás comer pechuga de pollo, cero muslos y alas** = You can only eat chicken breasts, no thighs or wings

- **Te recomiendo comenzar a comer pescado** = I recommend starting to eat fish

- **Una lata pequeña de atún con vegetales, con galletas tipo cracker** = A small can of tuna with vegetables and crackers

- **Plato de avena con canela** = Bowl of oatmeal with cinnamon

- **Sin azúcar** = Zero sugar

- **Gimnasio** = Gym

Spanish

Martin: Hola Erika, ¿por qué estás tan triste? Se te ve en la cara que no estás bien.

Erika: Oh, hola Martin. Lo que pasa es que estoy deprimida... Estoy cansada de tener esta figura, ¡ya no aguanto! **Siento que estoy muy obesa**; ya **no puedo correr por largas distancias, todo el tiempo pienso en comer**, mi esposo ya no me mira igual, y la ropa ya no me queda.

Martin: ¡Qué mal! Pero sabes que todo eso lo puedes cambiar de un momento a otro, ¿no? Todo está en ti. Recuerda que soy doctor, y que te puedo ayudar.

Erika: Es cierto, Martin. **Eres nutricionista**, aunque muchas veces lo olvido. ¿De qué manera me recomiendas empezar?

Martin: Bueno, a pesar de que eres mi amiga, **no conozco tus hábitos de salud**. A ver, **¿cuántas veces a la semana sales a hacer algún tipo de ejercicio o actividad continua?**

Erika: Bueno, **tres veces a la semana** paseo a mi perro por una hora. Mi hermana lo hace el resto del tiempo. Y también camino a la estación del metro cada mañana y de vuelta al terminar mi jornada.

Martin: No es suficiente. **Necesitas sacar tiempo para ejercitarte y hacer al menos una hora de actividad fuerte diaria**, además de caminar más durante el día. ¿Quieres bajar de peso, no?

Erika: Sí. También **me gustaría saber qué tipo de dieta necesitaría hacer para poder comenzar a perder estos kilos** de más. Ya estoy decidida a cambiar mi vida, y haré lo que sea necesario.

Martin: Bueno, lo primero que hay que saber — **¿comes muchos alimentos con harina de trigo? ¿Consumes azúcares en altas cantidades? ¿Tienes un consumo moderado de alimentos fritos, y comida rápida?**

Erika: Ehh, la verdad que sí como bastantes alimentos a base de harina de trigo. Los dulces me encantan, y casi todos los días como chocolate o postres de algún tipo. **Trato de no comer comida rápida, aunque tomo muchas bebidas carbonatadas**, así sepa que no son buenas para mí.

Martin: Esta dieta no te será fácil entonces, Erika. Verás, **la harina de trigo no te está aportando los nutrientes**, sino que está sirviendo únicamente para llenar tu estómago. Por esta razón, **no estás alimentándote bien. Los azúcares no sólo llevan hasta un incremento de peso, sino que pueden traer problemas de azúcar en la sangre y una probabilidad más alta de sufrir del corazón.** Cuando se trata de las bebidas carbonatadas, estas tienen una cantidad tan alta de azúcar, que te impresionarías — todo esto está causando que aumentes de peso y te sientas mal.

Erika: Entonces, ¿qué me recomiendas? Si quieres puedes cobrarme por esta consulta. ¡Necesito saber!

Martin: De acuerdo, **necesitas comenzar primero con eliminar los azúcares. Trata de comer frutas,** las cuales también tienen azúcar, pero que son sanas y aportan otros nutrientes a tu organismo. Segundo, **vas a intentar comer menos calorías en cada comida, pero tratar de comer más veces.** Es decir, **puedes comer cinco veces al día,** pero sólo si son **comidas ligeras** y **con vegetales crudos.** ¿Me estás siguiendo?

Erika: Sí, ya estoy tomando nota en mi teléfono celular. Vegetales crudos... Sí, continúa. ¿Qué tal mis postres?

Martin: Elimínalos. Comienza comiendo sólo un postre semanal, pero eventualmente trata de que no comas ninguno. De todas maneras, una vez hayas reducido considerablemente tu consumo de azúcar, tu cuerpo no querrá consumirla. Ah, **trata de cocinar tus alimentos a la plancha o hervirlos. No utilices aceite ni grasa para cocinar.** Esto mejorará tu salud considerablemente. ¿Comes carne, pollo o cerdo?

Erika: Sí, me encanta comer carne, pollo y especialmente cerdo.

Martin: Trata de no comer cerdo. Tiene mucha grasa. Si vas a comer carne, que sean **cortes sin grasa,** y siempre a la plancha. **Sólo podrás comer pechuga de pollo, cero muslos y alas. Te recomiendo comenzar a comer pescado. Una lata pequeña de atún con vegetales, con galletas tipo cracker** puede ser tu cena esta noche. Un desayuno mañana puede ser un **plato de avena con canela. Sin azúcar.**

Erika: Eso no suena tan divertido. ¿No puedo comer huevo frito con tocineta?

Martin: En lo absoluto. Voy a recomendarte que te metas a un

gimnasio. Ahora sí, ve con calma. Nada va a ser instantáneo, y puede que necesites varias semanas para ver algún resultado. Pero funcionará.

Erika: Excelente, Doctor Martin. Esta consulta valió la pena. ¿Algo más?

Martin: No, más nada. Si quieres me pagas con un café y un sandwich y estamos bien.

Erika: ¡Excelente! ¡Vamos entonces!

English

Martin: Hello Erika, why do you look so sad? It's clear on your face that you're not feeling well.

Erika: Oh, hello Martin. It's just that I feel depressed... I'm tired of having this body shape, I can't stand it anymore! **I feel that I'm too obese; I can't run for long distances anymore, I think of eating all day**, my husband doesn't look at me the same way, and my clothes don't fit anymore.

Martin: That's terrible! But you know that all of that can change from one moment to the next, right? It's all up to you. Remember that I'm a doctor, and that I can help you.

Erika: That's true, Martin. **You're a nutritionist**, although many times I forget. How should I start?

Martin: Well, despite the fact that you're my friend, **I don't know your health habits**. Let's see, **how many times a week do you go out to get some exercise or continuous physical activity?**

Erika: Let's see, **three times a week** I walk my dog for an hour. My sister does it the rest of the time. I also walk to the train station every morning and back again once my shift is over.

Martin: That's not enough. **You need to make time to get exercise and spend at least one hour a day on strong activity**, as well as walking more during the day. You do want to lose weight, don't you?

Erika: Yes. **I would also like to know what kind of diet I need to do so that I can start losing these extra pounds.** I've decided to change my life, and I'm willing to do whatever I have to.

Martin: All right, the first thing I must know — **do you eat many different foods made from wheat flour? Do you eat large quantities of sugar? Do you have a moderate consumption of fried food and fast food?**

Erika: Uhh, I actually eat many things that are made out of wheat flour. I absolutely love sweets, and almost every day I eat chocolate or some kind of dessert. **I try not to eat fast food, although I drink many**

carbonated beverages, even though I know they're not good for me.

Martin: This diet won't be easy for you then, Erika. You see, **wheat flour isn't really giving you any nutrients,** as it is only serving to fill your stomach. For this precise reason, **you're not nourishing yourself properly**. **Sugars don't just lead to an increase in weight, but they also can cause problems with sugar in the blood**, as well as increase the chances of suffering of heart disease. When it comes to carbonated beverages, these have such a high level of sugar that you'd be amazed — all of this is causing you to increase your weight and feel **bad**.

Erika: So, what do you recommend? If you want you can charge me for this consultation. I need to know!

Martin: Fine, **you need to start by getting rid of sugars. Try to eat fruits**, they also have sugars, but they are healthy and provide other nutrients to your body. Next, **you're going to try to eat less calories in each meal** but **try to eat more times a day**. In other words, **you can eat five times a day**, but only if they're **light meals with uncooked vegetables**. Are you following me?

Erika: Yeah, I'm taking notes on my cell phone. Uncooked veggies... Ok, continue. What about my desserts?

Martin: Get rid of them. Start by eating only one dessert a week, but eventually try to not eat any at all. Anyway, once you have considerably reduced your sugar consumption, your body will no longer want any. Ah, **try to cook your meals grilled or boiled. Don't use oil or fat to cook**. This will improve your health considerably. Do you eat meat, chicken or pork?

Erika: Yes, I love eating meat, chicken and especially pork.

Martin: Try not to eat pork. It has a lot of fat. If you're going to eat meat, try to get **fatless cuts**, and always grilled. **You can only eat chicken breasts, no thighs or wings. I recommend starting to eat fish. A small can of tuna with vegetables and crackers** can be your dinner tonight. Breakfast tomorrow could be a **bowl of oatmeal with cinnamon. Zero sugar**.

Erika: That doesn't sound too fun. Can't I eat a fried egg with bacon?

Martin: Not at all. I'm going to recommend for you to get yourself into a **gym**. Now, go slowly and calmly. Nothing will be instantaneous, and it could be a few weeks before you see any results. But it will work.

Erika: Excellent, Doctor Martin. This consultation was worth it. Anything else?

Martin: No, nothing else. If you want you can pay me with a coffee and a sandwich and we're good.

Erika: Excellent! Let's go then!

CHAPTER 19

PHYSIOTHERAPIST
¡ME LESIONÉ! — I'M INJURED!

Vocabulary List

- **¡Me duele mucho!** = It hurts a lot!
- **Creo que le pasó algo a mi rodilla** = I think something happened to my knee
- **Siento la pierna tiesa, y me duele cuando trato de doblarla** = I can feel a stiffness in my leg, and it hurts when I try to bend it
- **Puede que tengas una lesión** = You may have an injury
- **Trata de no hacerme daño** = Try not to hurt me
- **Puedo ver el sitio acá donde su bota impactó con tu rodilla** = I can see the place here where his boot slammed into your knee
- **¿Puedes intentar flexionar la rodilla?** = Can you try flexing your knee?
- **Para ver hasta dónde llega el daño** = To see how far the damage goes
- **¡Creo que es una lesión bastante seria!** = I really think this could be a very severe injury!
- **Sala de resonancias magnéticas** = MRI room
- **Saber cómo se está comportando el tejido** = See how the tissue is behaving
- **Lesión del ligamento cruzado anterior** = Anterior cruciate ligament injury
- **Meses de recuperación** = Months of recovery
- **Flexionando un poco la rodilla** = Flex your knee a bit
- **Te vamos a revisar la rodilla** = Check on your knee
- **Sí tienes una inflamación** = You certainly do have swelling

- **Tienes una lesión en el ligamento posterior** = You have a posterior ligament injury
- **Vas a sentir dolor y sufrir de inflamación por otros días más** = You're going to feel pain and suffer from swelling for another few days

Spanish

Marco: ¡Ah! **¡Me duele mucho!**

Fernanda: ¿Qué? ¿Qué te sucede, Marco? ¿Estás bien?

Marco: No, para nada. En esas últimas jugadas del partido, **creo que le pasó algo a mi rodilla. Siento la pierna tiesa, y me duele cuando trato de doblarla.** Tiene algo que ver con la entrada del jugador contrario a los setenta minutos, seguramente.

Fernanda: Yo vi eso, y me parece que fue un poco brusco. **Puede que tengas una lesión**, lo mejor es que te acuestes para revisarte. Esperemos que no sea nada serio, ya que sabes que el tiempo de recuperación puede llegar a ser largo.

Marco: Sí, y estamos entrando en la parte más importante de la temporada. El equipo y el coach me necesitan para seguir anotando goles.

Fernanda: Sí, pero también tienes que pensar en un descanso para que esto no empeore. Acuéstate, por favor. Podemos hablar mientras te reviso.

Marco: ¡Ah! Cierto. A ver, **trata de no hacerme daño**, que me duele muchísimo.

Fernanda: No, tranquilo que estás en buenas manos. Mmm, sí, **puedo ver el sitio acá donde su bota impactó con tu rodilla.** Fue un golpe bastante fuerte, ¿no?

Marco: Sí, aunque no lo sentí así al momento. Todo pasó tan rápido, a una velocidad impresionante. No esperaba que fuera serio. Por eso seguí jugando, supongo.

Fernanda: Yo tampoco lo vi así tan serio. **¿Puedes intentar flexionar la rodilla?** Es **para ver hasta dónde llega el daño**. Así, sigue... vamos, ¿no puedes flexionar más?

Marco: ¡Ahh! ¡No! Duele mucho, ¡mucho! ¡De verdad **creo que es una lesión bastante seria**!

Fernanda: Vamos a ponerle hielo y esperar unos diez minutos. Luego de eso, quiero que pasemos por la **sala de resonancias magnéticas**.

Marco: ¿Resonancia qué?

Fernanda: Es una técnica que nos permite mirar dentro de tu pierna y **saber cómo se está comportando el tejido** para saber si existe una lesión o no. Tengo el presentimiento que esto podría ser una **lesión del ligamento cruzado anterior**, lo cual podría significar **meses de recuperación**. Necesitamos estar seguros si es eso, o si está ocurriendo otra cosa.

Marco: ¿Es en serio? Yo conozco esas lesiones, y son una de las peores cosas que le puede ocurrir a un futbolista. Puede que no vuelva a jugar al mismo nivel si esa es mi lesión. Espero que no, de verdad.

Fernanda: Aún tenemos que hacer el diagnóstico. No nos adelantemos. ¿Cómo te ha hecho sentir el hielo? ¿Mejor?

Marco: Sí, mejor. ¿Ya estamos listos para la resonancia?

Fernanda: Me parece que sí. Te ayudaré a caminar hasta la sala de resonancias. Trata de caminar normal, eso sí. Ok, **flexionando un poco la rodilla**... perfecto. Por aquí.

Marco: Está muy fría esta sala. Me está haciendo doler más la rodilla.

Fernanda: Sí, es porque necesita estar a esta temperatura. Debes desvestirte y ponerte esta bata; te vamos a hacer pasar por la máquina que ves acá.

Marco: ¡Pero si soy claustrofóbico!

Fernanda: Lo que importa es que **te vamos a revisar la rodilla**. No tienes otra opción, así que aguántate.

Marco: De acuerdo, pero esto va a ser terrible para mí.

Fernanda: Tranquilízate, respira, y todo será rápido. En diez segundos comenzará la prueba. De acuerdo, estamos comenzando, puedes cerrar los ojos si lo deseas.

Marco: No, no hace falta. Bueno, ¿ya estás viendo mi rodilla? ¿Qué te parece?

Fernanda: Un momento, Marco. Estoy estudiando el área primero. **Sí tienes una inflamación**. Quiero mirar más a fondo.

Marco: Está bien, mira todo lo que necesites. Ya se me quitó la claustrofobia. De hecho, mi fobia más grande es una lesión de muchos meses, además de no jugar por todo ese tiempo.

Fernanda: Ya me imagino. Bueno Marco, ya estamos culminando las pruebas que teníamos que hacer. ¿Necesitas ayuda para salir de allí, o puedes sólo?

Marco: Puedo pararme sólo, aunque no está fácil. No te preocupes, que voy a tener que caminar de todas formas.

Fernanda: De acuerdo, te espero en la oficina acá. Voy a organizar la información.

Marco: Ya, por fin estoy en tu oficina.

Fernanda: ¡Que rápido! Toma asiento, que tengo noticias.

Marco: Oh... tengo mucho miedo.

Fernanda: Acá está el diagnóstico: no tienes una lesión del ligamento cruzado anterior. Esto deberá alegrarte mucho, y lo sé.

Marco: ¡Sí! ¡Genial! Estoy muy feliz de saberlo, pero cuénteme, ¿qué es lo que tengo?

Fernanda: Tienes una lesión en el ligamento posterior, pero no es nada seria. Eso sí, **vas a sentir dolor y sufrir de inflamación por otros días más.** Recomiendo que el director técnico te deje fuera por otras tres semanas. No será mucho, y podrás recuperarte por completo.

Marco: ¡Claro! No hay problema con tres semanas de recuperación. Muchas gracias, doctora. En serio no sabe lo feliz que estoy.

Fernanda: Sí lo sé. Ahora, ve a casa y recupérate. Todo estará bien, Marco. El equipo podrá sin ti. ¡Ánimo!

English

Marco: Ah! **It hurts a lot!**

Fernanda: What? What happened, Marco? Are you okay?

Marco: No, not at all. During the last moments of the game, **I think something happened to my knee. I can feel a stiffness in my leg, and it hurts when I try to bend it.** It surely has something to do with the tackle from the opposing player around the seventieth minute.

Fernanda: I saw that, and I believe that it was quite harsh. **You may have an injury**; the best thing to do is for you to lie down so I can check. Let's hope it isn't anything serious, because you know that the recovery time could be long.

Marco: Yeah, and we're about to enter the most crucial part of the season. The team and the coach need me there to keep scoring goals.

Fernanda: Yes, but you also have to think of a rest so that this doesn't worsen. Lie down, please. We can keep talking while I check this out.

Marco: Ah, sure. Let's see, **try not to hurt me**, because I'm feeling a lot of pain.

Fernanda: No, don't worry, you're in good hands. Mmm, yes, **I can see the place here where his boot slammed into your knee.** It was a very strong blow, wasn't it?

Marco: Yes, although it didn't feel that way at the time. Everything happened so quickly, at an impressive speed. I didn't expect it to be serious. That's why I kept on playing, I guess.

Fernanda: I didn't think it was that serious, either. **Can you try flexing your knee?** It's **to see how far the damage goes.** Okay, continue... come on, can't you flex it any further?

Marco: Ahh! No! It hurts so much, *so much!* **I really think this could be a very severe injury!**

Fernanda: Let's put some ice on it and wait about ten minutes. After that, I want us to take a trip to the **MRI room.**

Marco: MR... what?

Fernanda: It's a technique used so that we can look inside your leg and **see how the tissue is behaving** so that we can determine if there is an injury or not. I have a feeling that this could be an **anterior cruciate ligament injury**, which could translate into **months of recovery**. We need to be sure of this, or if it's something else that happened.

Marco: Are you serious? I know these injuries, and they're one of the worst things that can happen to a football player. I may never play at my current level again if that's the case here. I hope it's not, for real.

Fernanda: We still have to make a diagnostic. Let's not get ahead of ourselves. How has the ice made you feel, better?

Marco: Yes, better. Are we ready for the MRI yet?

Fernanda: I believe we are. I'll help you walk to the MRI room. Try walking normally, like that. Ok, **flex your knee a bit**... perfect. Through here.

Marco: This room is very cold. It's making my knee hurt even more.

Fernanda: Yes, it's because it has to be at this temperature. You have to undress and put this robe on; I'm going to have you pass through this machine here.

Marco: But I'm claustrophobic!

Fernanda: What matters here is that we're going to **check on your knee**. You have no other option, so bear with it.

Marco: All right, but this is going to be terrible for me.

Fernanda: Calm down, breathe, and everything will be quick. In ten seconds, we'll begin the test. Very well, we're starting; you can close your eyes if you wish to.

Marco: No, I don't think I'll need to. Okay, are you looking at my knee? What do you think?

Fernanda: One moment, Marco. I'm studying the area first. **You certainly do have swelling**. I want to see more.

Marco: All right, look all you need to. The claustrophobic feeling is wearing off. In fact, my biggest phobia is an injury of several months, as well as not being to play for all that time.

Fernanda: I can imagine. Very well, Marco, we've concluded the tests we had to perform. Do you need help to get out of there, or can you do it on your own?

Marco: I can get up on my own, although it isn't easy right now. Don't worry, I'm going to have to learn to walk anyway.

Fernanda: All right, I'll expect you in the office over here. I'm going to organize my findings.

Marco: Here, I'm finally in your office.

Fernanda: That was quick! Take a seat, I have news for you.

Marco: Oh... I'm feeling very afraid right now.

Fernanda: Here's the diagnostic: you don't have an anterior cruciate ligament injury. This should make you really happy and I know it.

Marco: Yes! Awesome! I'm very happy to know that, but tell me, what is it that I have instead?

Fernanda: You have a posterior ligament injury, but it isn't serious at all. That said, **you're going to feel pain and suffer from swelling for another few days**. I recommend that the manager leaves you out of action for another three weeks. It won't be much, and you'll be able to fully recover.

Marco: Of course! There isn't any problem with three weeks of recovery. Thanks a lot, doctor. You really have no idea how happy I am right now.

Fernanda: I actually do. Now, go home and recover. Everything will be okay, Marco. The team will manage without you. Godspeed!

CHAPTER 20

FIELD MEDIC

LOS HORRORES DE LA GUERRA — THE HORRORS OF WAR

Vocabulary List

- **Campo de batalla** = Battlefield
- **Heridos en los bombardeos** = Wounded in the bombings
- **Sangrienta** = Bloody
- **Soldados caídos de ambos lados** = Fallen soldiers on both sides
- **Personas con brazos o piernas amputadas** = People with missing arms and legs
- **Heridas de bala y/o cuchillos** = Bullet and/or knife wounds
- **Víctimas directas e indirectas de explosiones** = Direct and indirect explosion victims
- **Revolverme el estómago** = My stomach is already churning
- **Civiles caídos** = Fallen civilians
- **Esa persona se está moviendo** = That person is moving
- **¡Agarra su brazo izquierdo, yo haré lo mismo con el derecho!** = Grab the person's left arm, I'll do the same thing with their right!
- **Una herida en el pecho** = Wound in his chest
- **Tiene un pulmón perforado** = He has a pierced lung
- **Voy a limpiar su herida y tratar de cerrarla** = Clean his wound and try to seal it shut
- **Heridas de metralla** = Shrapnel wounds
- **Voy a extraerte estos terribles pedazos de metal** = I'm going to pull out those terrible pieces of metal

- **Recibió un disparo en la pierna** = He received a shot to the leg
- **La bala parece estar alojada cerca de la arteria femoral** = The bullet seems to be lodged near his femoral artery
- **Alcohol etílico** = Ethyl alcohol
- **Sufrieron de fracturas** = They suffered from fractures
- **Hombro dislocado** = Dislocated shoulder
- **Suero fisiológico** = Saline solution
- **Tratamiento para quemaduras** = Burn treatment
- **Condiciones reales de higiene** = Proper hygiene conditions

Spanish

Michael: Gabriella, voy a necesitar que estés lista en cinco minutos.

Gabriella: ¿Y eso por qué, teniente? ¿Qué sucede?

Michael: Saldremos al **campo de batalla** a ayudar a aquellos civiles que han sido **heridos en los bombardeos**, así dándoles un segundo chance a esos pobres inocentes que no merecían nada de esto. Ya va, ¿alguna vez has hecho esto antes? Tienes una cara de terror.

Gabriella: Sí, lo he hecho antes, pero esta guerra se ha tornado tan **sangrienta** y cruel que no quiero imaginar lo que vamos a encontrar allá afuera. Temo ver lo peor de la guerra que tanto me han hablado.

Michael: Y nada de lo que te contaron dice lo que realmente es la guerra. Es el infierno sobre la tierra, y puede servir para que entiendas lo absurdo que es el conflicto armado entre dos grupos de seres humanos.

Gabriella: Sí que lo es. No entiendo cómo dos naciones pueden matarse de esta manera.

Michael: Bueno, hablaremos luego de esto. Vamos, el vehículo ya vino por nosotros. ¿Estás lista?

Gabriella: Sí, estoy completamente lista. Ya tengo mi equipo y me tranquilicé un poco. ¿Hacia dónde vamos, específicamente?

Michael: Vamos hacia el este, donde la pelea se adentró en la ciudad. Puede que haya también **soldados caídos de ambos lados**. Sálvalos si deseas, pero primero los civiles. Bueno, ya salgamos para allá.

Gabriella: ¿Qué puedo esperar encontrar allá? Imagino que veré cosas terribles.

Michael: Así será. Habrá **personas con brazos o piernas amputadas, heridas de bala y/o cuchillos** y **víctimas directas e indirectas de explosiones**.

Gabriella: Eso suena terrible, hasta el punto de **revolverme el estómago**. Pero no importa, porque para eso estoy acá. Necesito salvar vidas.

Michael: Esa es la actitud. Ya estamos cerca, así que prepara tus cosas y tu mente para las experiencias que vienen. Mira, ya veo a los primeros **civiles caídos**. Vamos a ver si hay alguien que pueda salvarse.

Gabriella: Perfecto. ¡Hola! ¿Hay alguien con vida acá? ¡¿Hola?! Nadie, pareciera que… un momento, parece que **esa persona se está moviendo**.

Michael: Sí, ¡acerquémonos! Está tratando de salirse de la pila de cadáveres. Lo ayudaremos. **¡Agarra su brazo izquierdo, yo haré lo mismo con el derecho!**

Gabriella: De acuerdo. ¿Señor? Reaccione, que vinimos a salvarlo y necesitamos saber si está bien. ¿Señor?

Michael: No responde. Bueno, al menos está vivo, ¿no? Creo…

Gabriella: Sí está vivo. Pero tenemos que seguir buscando entre este cerro de caídos para saber con certeza si no existe otra persona viva.

Michael: Probablemente no, Gabriella. Vamos a atenderlo a él mientras podamos, y luego pasamos adelante con el restante de las víctimas. Mmm… parece tener **una herida en el pecho**. ¿Puedes ver hasta dónde llega el daño?

Gabriella: **Tiene un pulmón perforado**, y eso es bastante preocupante. **Voy a limpiar su herida y tratar de cerrarla** al menos, eso podría darle una oportunidad mientras llega la salvación.

Michael: ¿Listo? Vamos con los siguientes, que puedo ver un grupo de personas allá detrás de esa pared.

Gabriella: De acuerdo. Bueno, esta joven tiene **heridas de metralla** por estar muy cerca a una bomba cuando explotó. Cálmate chica, **voy a extraerte estos terribles pedazos de metal**. Falta poco, aguanta… ¡Listo!

Michael: Excelente trabajo, ahora encarguémonos de este soldado baleado.

Gabriella: Sí, ya veo. **Recibió un disparo en la pierna, y la bala parece estar alojada cerca de la arteria femoral**. ¿Puede ayudarme a extraerla?

Michael: Lo intentaré, pero primero tenemos que anestesiarlo. Le daré esto que tengo guardado de hace tiempo.

Gabriella: ¡Pero si es **alcohol etílico**! Bueno, será… Aguanta el dolor, amigo, ya estoy haciendo lo que debo hacer.

Michael: Acá hay unos ancianos que me necesitan. Parece que se les derrumbó la casa y **sufrieron de fracturas**. ¿Puedes sola?

Gabriella: Sí. Bueno, ya estoy lista. ¡Necesitamos apoyo, son demasiados!

Michael: El apoyo está muy lejos aún. ¿Puedes ayudarme a poner este **hombro dislocado** de vuelta en su lugar?

Gabriella: Ok, uno, dos y tres… Vaya, no fue fácil. Voy a darles un poco de **suero fisiológico** para que se rehidraten. Los bombarderos están acabando con todo, ¡me parte el alma ver los destrozos y daño que causan!

Michael: Así es la guerra. Les quita a todos por igual, y los de arriba se llevan la mejor parte. Mira, unos niños están pidiendo ayuda. Creo que lograron salir de un incendio en esa casa. ¿Tienes **tratamiento para quemaduras**?

Gabriella: ¡Esto pareciera que jamás va a acabar! Sí, si tengo. Vamos a ayudarlos. Oye, ¿qué es ese sonido?

Michael: Es un helicóptero. ¡Es de los nuestros, ya viene el apoyo! Vamos, trata de ayudar a los niños a caminar para que puedan llevarlos a la capital y tratarlos allá.

Gabriella: Sí, es lo mejor que podemos hacer, para que sean tratados en **condiciones reales de higiene**. Niños, ¡con nosotros!

English

Michael: Gabriella, I'm going to need you ready in five minutes.

Gabriella: Why is that, captain? What's going on?

Michael: We're going out to the **battlefield** to help those civilians that have been **wounded in the bombings**, allowing those poor innocents to have a second chance after not deserving any of this that is going on. Wait, haven't you ever done this before? You have a look of terror on your face.

Gabriella: Yes, I have done this before, but this war has turned so **bloody** and cruel that I don't want to imagine what we're going to find out there. I fear seeing the worst of this war that I've been told so much about.

Michael: And nothing that they told you is what war really looks like. It's hell on Earth, and it can serve as a lesson for you to see how absurd armed conflict is between two groups of human beings.

Gabriella: It certainly is. I don't understand how two nations can kill each other in such a way.

Michael: Well, we can talk later about this. Come, the vehicle has already come for us. Are you ready?

Gabriella: Yes, I'm absolutely ready. I have my equipment and I've calmed down. Where are we going, specifically?

Michael: We're going east, where the fighting went far into the city. There may be **fallen soldiers on both sides**. Save them if you wish, but first the civilians. Well, it's time to go.

Gabriella: What can I expect to witness there? I can guess that I'll see terrible things.

Michael: You definitely will. There will be **people with missing arms and legs, bullet and/or knife wounds**, and both **direct and indirect explosion victims**.

Gabriella: That sounds horrible, to the point where **my stomach is already churning**. But it doesn't matter, because that's what I'm here for. I need to save lives.

Michael: That's the spirit. We're getting closer, so prepare your things and your mind for the experiences you're about to go through. Look, I can see the first **fallen civilians.** Let's see if there's anyone left that can be saved.

Gabriella: Perfect. Hello! Is there anyone alive left here? Hello?! Nobody, it looks like... wait a moment, it looks like **that person is moving**.

Michael: Yes, let's approach! They're trying to push their way out of the pile of corpses. We can help them. **Grab the person's left arm, I'll do the same thing with their right!**

Gabriella: Okay. Sir? Wake up, we've come to save you and need to know if you're okay. Sir?

Michael: He's not responding. Well, at least he's alive, right? I think...

Gabriella: Yes, he's alive. But we have to continue searching among this mound of fallen to know with certainty if there isn't another survivor.

Michael: Probably not, Gabriella. Let's tend to him while we can, and then we continue forward with the rest of the victims. Hmm... he seems to have a **wound in his chest**. Can you see the extent of the damage?

Gabriella: He has a pierced lung, and that is extremely worrying. I'm going to **clean his wound and try to seal it shut** at least, which may give him an opportunity while help arrives.

Michael: Done? Let's continue with the next victims, since I can see a group of people there behind that wall.

Gabriella: Very well. All right, this young lady has **shrapnel wounds** due to being very close to a bomb when it detonated. Calm down, girl, **I'm going to pull out those terrible pieces of metal**. Almost done, hold on... done!

Michael: Excellent work, we can now deal with this soldier who was shot.

Gabriella: Yeah, I can see. **He received a shot to the leg** and **the bullet seems to be lodged near his femoral artery**. Can you help me extract it?

Michael: I'll try, but first we need to put him to sleep. I'll give him this, which I had been saving for a while.

Gabriella: But that's **ethyl alcohol**! Well, it's going to have to do... Withstand the pain, buddy, I'm doing what I have to do.

Michael: There are some elderly people here that need me. It looks like their house collapsed and **they suffered from fractures**. Can you do this alone?

Gabriella: Yeah. Well, I'm done here. We need support, there are too many of them!

Michael: Our support is still too far away. Can you help me put this **dislocated shoulder** back in its place?

Gabriella: Ok, one, two and three... Wow, it wasn't that easy. I'm going to provide them with a bit of **saline solution** so that they can be rehydrated. The bomber planes are destroying everything, it really breaks my heart to see the destruction and derby that they cause!

Michael: That's just how war is. It takes from everyone equally, and the ones on top take the best part of it. Look, some kids are asking for help. I think they managed to get out of a fire in that house. Do you have **burn treatment**?

Gabriella: It's like this is never going to end! Yes, yes I do. We're going to help them. Hey, what's that noise?

Michael: It's a helicopter. It's one of our own, support is coming! Come on, let's try to help the kids walk so that we can take them to the capital and treat them there.

Gabriella: Yes, it's the best we could do, so that they can be treated in **proper hygiene conditions**. Children, with us!

CHAPTER 21

COMATOSE PATIENT
PACIENCIA Y FORTALEZA —
PATIENCE AND FORTITUDE

Vocabulary List

- **Este estado** = This state
- **La cantidad de alcohol que consumía en su vida diaria** = Of his daily alcohol consumption
- **Grupo de ayuda** = Help group
- **Las personas que se encuentran en coma sí pueden escuchar las cosas a su alrededor** = People who are under a coma can listen to things around them
- **¿Cómo va a ayudarlo escucharme hablar así en coma?** = How is it going to help him talking to him like that while he's in a coma?
- **¿Cuánto tiempo crees que dure en coma?** = How long do you think he could be in a coma?
- **¿Algún día volverá a caminar, correr, portarse bien o mal?** = Will he ever go back to walking, running, behaving good or bad?
- **Puede que sean días, semanas o meses** = It may be days, weeks or months
- **Desvanecidos por largos meses** = Faded away for long months
- **Este tipo de acontecimiento puede afectar el cerebro de alguna forma u otra** = This kind of event can affect the brain in several ways
- **Es bastante difícil despertar de esta situación, e igual de difícil volver a la normalidad** = It is quite difficult to wake up from that situation, and it can be even harder to return to normality
- **El cerebro puede sufrir las consecuencias** = The brain can suffer

the consequences

- **Puede que haya degradación en la capacidad motora del paciente** = There could be degradation in the patient's motor ability

- **Voy a recetar una dieta y un tratamiento médico para tu papá** = I'm going to prescribe a diet and a medical treatment for your dad

- **Ahora en adelante vas a tener que cuidar su salud** = You're going to have to take care of his health from now on

- **Este estado es muy delicado** = This state is very delicate

- **Presta atención y síguelo todo al pie de la letra** = Pay attention and follow it all to the letter

Spanish

Jonas: No puedo creer que mi padre llegara a **este estado**, en estas condiciones y sin que yo pueda estar seguro de que va a sobrevivir a lo que viene. Parece algo de una de mis peores pesadillas.

Katherine: Entiendo tu dolor y decepción, pero esto es consecuencia de **la cantidad de alcohol que consumía en su vida diaria**. Muchas veces le exigí que dejara la bebida, e incluso lo obligué a entrar a un **grupo de ayuda**, pero nunca me prestó mucha atención.

Jonas: Sí, recuerdo el año pasado que estuvo en ese grupo un tiempo. No tengo idea de lo que hablaban allí, pero le hacía muy bien. Aunque al parecer no le hizo tanto bien, sino no estuviera acá en esta cama, sin saber qué está ocurriendo alrededor de él.

Katherine: Hay evidencias de que **las personas que se encuentran en coma sí pueden escuchar las cosas a su alrededor**, así que no dudes de lo bien que le estás haciendo al tomarlo en cuenta a pesar de su enfermedad. En cuanto al grupo de autoayuda, se trata de eso mismo: de que se ayuden ellos mismos.

Jonas: Entiendo. Es cierto, mi padre jamás quiso integrarse en sociedades, por lo cual enteendería si este nunca fue un grupo de autoayuda para personas como él. Si dices que debo ayudarlo, ¿qué debería decirle?

Katherine: Recuérdale lo que sientes por él; déjale claro que lo amas a pesar de sus errores.

Jonas: Y ¿cómo va a ayudarlo escucharme hablar así en coma?

Katherine: Puede que se esfuerce más por regresar a este mundo real, y que escuche las palabras que tiene años queriendo oír. Además: no pierdes nada por intentarlo.

Jonas: No, es cierto. A ver, **¿cuánto tiempo crees que dure en coma? ¿Algún día volverá a caminar, correr, portarse bien o mal?** Siempre fue un hombre activo, así que para él sería una tortura que no pudiera hacer nada sin ayuda.

Katherine: Sólo el tiempo podrá decirlo, Jonas. Recuerda que algunos son más fuertes que otros. **Puede que sean días, semanas o meses.** Ni siquiera tiene que ver con el dinero que inviertes en la recuperación. Hasta los más millonarios han sufrido de comas y han estado **desvanecidos por largos meses.** En cuanto a correr, caminar y lo demás… no es fácil, porque **este tipo de acontecimiento puede afectar el cerebro de alguna forma u otra.**

Jonas: ¿Qué me quieres decir, entonces? ¿Ya perdí a mi papá como lo conocí? ¿Será otro hombre el que despierte de este coma?

Katherine: Sólo en las películas y series de televisión verás personas que se paran de un coma y ya saben cómo llegaron ahí y con quién deben irse. En la vida real, **es bastante difícil despertar de esta situación, e igual de difícil volver a la normalidad. El cerebro puede sufrir las consecuencias, y puede que haya degradación en la capacidad motora del paciente.**

Jonas: Trataré de ayudarlo lo más que pueda, siempre teniendo la paciencia necesaria si necesita ser recordado sobre algo, y hacerle los favores que necesite para su vida diaria.

Katherine: Sí, Jonas. Necesitas tener paciencia e ir paso a paso. Sobre la pregunta que me hiciste sobre encontrarte con un hombre distinto a tu padre, es posible. Todo es posible ahora. **Voy a recetar una dieta y un tratamiento médico para tu papá,** ya que de **ahora en adelante vas a tener que cuidar su salud.** ¿Bien? **Este estado es muy delicado,** y debemos estar agradecidos que no terminó peor.

Jonas: Excelente, ¿qué debo hacer?

Katherine: Ya te lo voy a escribir. **Presta atención y síguelo todo al pie de la letra.** No queremos errores.

Jonas: Sí, ¡está bien!

English

Jonas: I can't believe that my father ended up in **this state** and in these conditions. I'm not feeling sure that he'll survive what's coming. It seems like something from my worst nightmares.

Katherine: I understand your pain and disappointment, but this is a consequence **of his daily alcohol consumption.** I tried to help him quit drinking many times, and I even forced him to enter a **help group**, but he never paid me much attention.

Jonas: Yes, I remember that last year he was in that group for a time. I have no idea of what exactly they spoke about there, but it did him well. Though apparently it didn't do him that well, considering he's lying here in this bed, without a single idea of what's going on around him.

Katherine: There is evidence that **people who are under a coma can listen to things around them**, so don't question the good that you'd be doing for him by paying him attention despite his illness. As for the self-help group, it's all about that: members helping themselves.

Jonas: I understand. It's true, my father never wanted to make himself part of societies, which is why I'd understand if it was never a self-help group for people like him. If you say I have to help him, what exactly should I tell him?

Katherine: Remind him what you feel for him; make it clear for him that you love him despite his mistakes.

Jonas: And, **how is it going to help him talking to him like that while he's in a coma?**

Katherine: He may fight harder to return back to the real world, as well as listen to those words he's been waiting to hear for years. Anyway, you won't lose anything for trying.

Jonas: No, it's true. Let's see, **how long do you think he could be in a coma? Will he ever go back to walking, running, behaving good or bad?** He was always an active man, so for him it would be a torture that he couldn't do anything on his own.

Katherine: Only time will tell, Jonas. Remember that some people are stronger than others. **It may be days, weeks or months**. It doesn't even have to do with the money you invest in his recovery. Even the biggest millionaires have suffered from comas and have **faded away for long months**. When it comes to the running, walking and everything else... it won't be easy, because **this kind of event can affect the brain in several ways**.

Jonas: What are you trying to tell me then? That I lost the father that I knew? That he'll be another man once he awakes from this coma?

Katherine: Only in movies and TV series will you ever see somebody get up from a coma and know how they got there and with whom to leave. In real life, **it is quite difficult to wake up from that situation, and it can be even harder to return to normality. The brain can suffer the consequences, and there could be degradation in the patient's motor ability**.

Jonas: I will try to help him as much as I can, always being patient enough to remind him about what he needs to know, and help with any favors he requires for his daily tasks.

Katherine: Yes, Jonas. You will need patience and step by step progress. Regarding what you asked about him being a different man once he awakes, it is possible Everything is possible now. **I'm going to prescribe a diet and a medical treatment for your dad**, because **you're going to have to take care of his health from now on**. Okay? **This state is very delicate**, and we must be thankful that it didn't end up worse.

Jonas: Excellent, what should I do?

Katherine: I'm going to write that now. **Pay attention and follow it all** to the letter. We don't want any mistakes.

Jonas: Yes, fine!

CHAPTER 22

WILD ANIMAL ATTACK
LAS GARRAS DE LA FIERA —
THE CLAWS OF THE BEAST

Vocabulary List

- **¡Sé que es tarde, pero necesitamos de su ayuda!** = I know it's late, but we need your help!
- **¡A mi hermana la acaba de atacar un animal salvaje en el bosque!** = She was just attacked by a wild animal in the forest!
- **Un salvaje y peligroso oso de la nada, con sus garras al aire y sus poderosos rugidos!** = Dangerous, wild bear came out of nowhere, with its claws in the air and its powerful roars!
- **Podrían atacarla otros animales que huelan su sangre** = She could be attacked by other animals that smell her blood
- **Lo que pueda haber ahí tratando de comerse a tu hermana** = Whatever is out there trying to eat your sister
- **Abre mi kit de medicinas para buscar alcohol isopropílico y vendajes** = Open my medical kit so you can look for isopropyl alcohol and bandages
- **¡Trate de subir rápido, o me voy a lesionar!** = Try to climb quickly, or I'm going to get hurt!
- **No se ve muy bien** = She doesn't look well
- **Vamos a tener que ir al hospital en mi auto** = We're going to have to go to the hospital in my car
- **Tiene una herida profunda, y está sangrando profusamente** = She has a deep wound, and it's bleeding profusely
- **Déjame echar alcohol en su herida y limpiarla** = Let me put some alcohol in her wound and clean it

- **Trata de que no grite** = Try not to let her scream
- **La herida está fea, pero se puede tratar antes de ir al hospital** = The wound is ugly, but it can be treated before we head out to the hospital
- **Necesito buscar algodón, y algo de adhesivo médico para la gaza** = I need to get some cotton, and some medical tape for the gauze
- **Que garras tan afiladas tiene el oso, causó una cortada enorme en la piel** = The bear had really sharp claws, which caused an enormous cut
- **Vamos a morir** = We're going to die
- **Cuida bien a tu hermana** = Take care of your sister

Spanish

Regina: ¡Auxilio! ¡Doctor Albert, Doctor Albert! ¡Salga pronto, venga ya! **¡Sé que es tarde, pero necesitamos de su ayuda!**

Albert: ¿Qué, qué pasa? ¿Qué quieres? Estaba durmiendo, ¡son las dos de la mañana, Regina!

Regina: ¡Sí, lo sé, lo sé! ¡Pero es que **a mi hermana la acaba de atacar un animal salvaje en el bosque!**

Albert: Ya va, ¿estoy escuchando bien? ¿Un animal salvaje?

Regina: Sí, estábamos caminando por un sendero para ver las estrellas de noche y fotografiar el cielo, ¡y nos salió **un salvaje y peligroso oso de la nada, con sus garras al aire y sus poderosos rugidos!** Está muy mal, pero tuve que dejarla sola en un árbol para venir a buscarlo...

Albert: Así que está allá afuera completamente sola. Eso si es malo, **podrían atacarla otros animales que huelan su sangre.**

Regina: Pero está en un árbol, doctor.

Albert: ¿Y qué? ¿Acaso no sabes que los osos pueden escalar árboles? Necesitamos ir; déjame ponerme unas botas, buscar la linterna y un kit médico. Ah, y un rifle por si acaso.

Regina: Sí, buena idea. ¡No sabía que podían escalar árboles! Ahora estoy más preocupada por ella. ¡En realidad si hubiese sabido eso no la hubiera dejado!

Albert: Sí, de verdad que no eres la más inteligente, pero tendremos que luchar con **lo que pueda haber ahí tratando de comerse a tu hermana.** Ya tengo lo que necesitaba, vamos. Trata de mantenerte a mi lado, puede que tenga que usar el rifle.

Regina: Eso sí me gustaría verlo.

Albert: ¡No es un juego! No es culpa del oso que ustedes estuvieran en su territorio husmeando.

Regina: No estábamos husmeando, sólo estábamos... era para subir las fotos al internet y ganar un concurso de fotografía.

Albert: Vaya, entiendo. Bueno, ya veremos si tendrás chance o no de ganar eso. Un momento, ¡silencio! Acabo de oír algo.

Regina: De acuerdo. Creo que es un oso.

Albert: No, no es un oso. Mmm... creo que era el viento. Sigamos.

Regina: ¡Ahí está mi hermana! ¡Jennifer! ¡Traje al doctor!

Albert: ¡Baja la voz, niña! Menos mal que está bien. Al parecer no han llegado los animales aun, pero debemos movernos antes de que lo hagan. Ayúdame a subir, y **abre mi kit de medicinas para buscar alcohol isopropílico y vendajes. ¡Rápido!**

Regina: Sí, sí. Déjame ayudarlo primero, doctor. Súbase acá. ¡Oye, pesa mucho! **¡Trate de subir rápido, o me voy a lesionar!**

Albert: No te quejes tanto, niña. Estoy tratando de ayudar. A ver, Jennifer, ¿te sientes bien? **No se ve muy bien**, Regina. Ten a mano lo que te pedí. **Vamos a tener que ir al hospital en mi auto; tiene una herida profunda, y está sangrando profusamente.** ¿Puedes cargarla mientras me bajo?

Regina: De acuerdo. Ven, Jennifer. No te caigas... Perfecto, ya te vamos a tratar y cuidar. Sólo aguanta.

Albert: Perfecto, **déjame echar alcohol en su herida y limpiarla. Trata de que no grite. La herida está fea, pero se puede tratar antes de ir al hospital.**

Regina: ¿Qué necesita? Puedo ayudarlo.

Albert: Aguanta acá, **necesito buscar algodón, y algo de adhesivo médico para la gaza.** Mmm... ya, aquí está. **Que garras tan afiladas tiene el oso, causó una cortada enorme en la piel** de Jennifer.

Regina: ¿Pero va a estar bien?

Albert: Sí. Un momento... Regina, quédate muy quieta, y esta vez es en serio.

Regina: ¿Qué pasa?

Albert: El oso... parece que ha regresado. No grites, por más que quieras. Necesitamos irnos lentamente, así que carga bien a tu hermana. Yo necesito tener el rifle a mano.

Regina: **Vamos a morir**.

Albert: No vamos a morir, niña. Sólo **cuida bien a tu hermana**, y yo me encargo del resto. Oh, rayos. Ya nos vio.

Regina: ¿Corremos?

Albert: ¡Sí! ¡Corre! ¡Aléjate lo más que puedas! ¡Fuera de aquí, oso! Sígueme, Regina, mi auto está por acá. ¡Vamos!

Regina: Se está acercando, ¡dispárale!

Albert: Sí, ¡ya le disparé! Está huyendo. ¡Nos salvamos!

Regina: ¡Ya, vamos al hospital!

Albert: ¡Sí, vámonos ya!

English

Regina: Help! Doctor Albert, Doctor Albert! Come out quick, come now! **I know it's late, but we need your help!**

Albert: What, what's going on? What do you want? I was sleeping, it's two in the morning, Regina!

Regina: Yes, I know, I know! But it's my sister, **she was just attacked by a wild animal in the forest!**

Albert: Wait, am I listening clearly? A wild animal?

Regina: Yes, we were walking along a path to see the stars at night and take a picture of the sky, and a **dangerous, wild bear came out of nowhere, with its claws in the air and its powerful roars!** She's in very bad shape, but I had to leave her alone in a tree so that I could come and get you...

Albert: So she's out there completely alone. That really is bad; **she could be attacked by other animals that smell her blood.**

Regina: But she's in a tree, doctor.

Albert: So what? Don't you know that bears can climb trees? We need to go; let me put on my boots, grab a torch and a medical kit. Ah, and a rifle just in case.

Regina: Yes, good idea. I didn't know they could climb trees. Now I'm even more worried for her. I wouldn't have left her if I had known that!

Albert: Yeah, you're not the sharpest tool in the shed, but we're going to have to fight with **whatever is out there trying to eat your sister**. I have what I need, so let's go. Try to remain at my side, I may need to use the rifle.

Regina: That I'd like to see.

Albert: It's not a game! It's not the bear's fault that you were in its territory snooping around.

Regina: We weren't snooping, we were just... it was all to upload the photos to the internet and win a photography contest.

Albert: Wow, I see. Well, let's see if we have a chance for you to win that or not. One moment, silence! I just heard something.

Regina: All right. I think it's a bear.

Albert: No, it isn't a bear. Mmm... I think it was the wind. Let's continue.

Regina: There's my sister! Jennifer! I brought the doctor!

Albert: Lower your voice, girl! Thankfully she's okay. It seems that the animals haven't arrived yet, but we must get moving before they do. Help me up, and **open my medical kit so you can look for isopropyl alcohol and bandages**. Quick!

Regina: Yeah, yeah. Let me help you first, doctor. Hop on. Hey, you're heavy! **Try to climb quickly, or I'm going to get hurt!**

Albert: Don't complain so much, girl. I'm trying to help. Let's see, Jennifer, do you feel okay? **She doesn't look well**, Regina. Get the things that I told you ready. **We're going to have to go to the hospital in my car; she has a deep wound, and it's bleeding profusely.** Can you carry her while I climb down?

Regina: All right. Come, Jennifer. Don't fall... Perfect, we're going to treat and care for you now. Just hold on.

Albert: Perfect, **let me put some alcohol in her wound and clean it. Try not to let her scream. The wound is ugly, but it can be treated before we head out to the hospital.**

Regina: What do you need? I can help you.

Albert: Hold on here, **I need to get some cotton, and some medical tape for the gauze**. Mmm... here, that's it. **The bear had really sharp claws, which caused an enormous cut** on Jennifer's skin.

Regina: But will she be okay?

Albert: Yes. One moment... Regina, stay very still, and this time it's for real.

Regina: What's up?

Albert: The bear... it looks like it's back. Don't scream whatever you do. We need to leave slowly, so carry your sister tightly. I need to have my rifle in hand.

Regina: We're going to die.

Albert: We're not going to die, girl. Just **take care of your sister**, and I'll be in charge of the rest. Oh, shoot. It's seen us.

Regina: Should we run?

Albert: Yes! Run! Get as far away as you can! Get out of here, bear! Follow me, Regina, my car is through here! Let's go!

Regina: It's getting closer, shoot it!

Albert: Yes, I just did! It's fleeing. We're saved!

Regina: Okay, let's go to the hospital!

Albert: Yes, let's go now!

CHAPTER 23

FORENSIC TESTING

UN MISTERIO SIN RESOLVER —
AN UNRESOLVED MYSTERY

Vocabulary List

- **¿Estás acá por el caso del asesinato en el callejón de Queens? =** Guess you're here for that murder case in the back alley in Queens?
- **Tipo de progreso has hecho con el cuerpo de la víctima =** What kind of progress you've made with the body of the victim
- **Quiero corroborar con lo que pudiste observar =** Want to verify what I know with what you've observed
- **Comencemos con mi análisis =** Let's begin with my analysis
- **Tenía alcohol en su sangre =** She had alcohol in her blood
- **Además de la vejiga llena =** As well as a full bladder
- **Su cuerpo no estaba en movimiento cuando recibió el primer golpe =** Her body wasn't in motion when she received her first blow
- **Fue un golpe descendiente con objeto contundente de metal en el hombro =** It was a descending blow on her shoulder with a blunt metal object
- **Apuntaron a su cráneo =** They aimed at her skull
- **El primer golpe y el empujón en el pecho que le siguió =** Her first blow and the shove in the chest that followed
- **Segundo golpe con el mismo objeto =** Second blow followed with the same object
- **Esta vez en su sien =** This time in her temple

- **Cambió el objeto contundente por una navaja corta** = Swapped the blunt object for a short knife
- **La apuñaló cinco veces** = He stabbed her five times
- **Una vez en el abdomen a la altura del páncreas** = Once in the abdomen around her pancreas
- **Otro en el brazo izquierdo, entre bíceps y tríceps** = Another in her left arm, between biceps and triceps
- **Otras tres en la garganta** = The other three times in her throat
- **Cortó su vena yugular** = Sliced the jugular vein
- **Haciendo que se desangrara** = Causing her to bleed to death
- **Muerte dolorosa y desesperante** = Painful and desperate death
- **Ni siquiera opuso tanta resistencia** = She didn't even show much resistance

Spanish

Stephen: ¿Qué onda, Lauren?

Lauren: Todo bien, Stephen. ¿Supongo que **estás acá por el caso del asesinato en el callejón de Queens**, no?

Stephen: Exactamente. Quería saber qué **tipo de progreso has hecho con el cuerpo de la víctima**. No quiero dar detalles, pero me han llegado informaciones un poco extrañas, por lo que **quiero corroborar con lo que pudiste observar**.

Lauren: Sí, entiendo. Nada es lo que parece, y a veces este tipo de casos nos puede caer de sorpresa, ¿no? Bueno, **comencemos con mi análisis**, para ver si tiene algún tipo de relación con tus descubrimientos.

Stephen: Perfecto, voy a comenzar a anotar mientras hablas. Seguramente tendré preguntas, así que prepárate.

Lauren: De acuerdo. Bueno, la víctima estaba caminando sola a esa hora, aproximadamente a las tres y quince de la mañana, parece que venía de una fiesta. Lo sé porque **tenía alcohol en su sangre, además de la vejiga llena.**

Stephen: ¿Piensas que estaba en un sitio donde no podía ir al baño, cierto? Buena observación.

Lauren: Eso mismo. Seguramente decidió tomar un atajo, tras lo que pasó por ese callejón donde se encontraría con la muerte.

Stephen: Sí, así también creo que fue.

Lauren: Caminó pocos metros, pero algo la hizo detenerse. **Su cuerpo no estaba en movimiento cuando recibió el primer golpe. Fue un golpe descendiente con objeto contundente de metal en el hombro.** Creo que **apuntaron a su cráneo**, pero ella pudo esquivarlo ligeramente. Eso no fue suficiente para tumbarla, pero aún así no intentó correr.

Stephen: ¿No intentó correr?

Lauren: No. De hecho, tengo una teoría sobre eso.

Stephen: Bueno, yo también tengo una. Ella conocía a su victimario.

Lauren: ¡Exactamente! Tras recibir **el primer golpe y el empujón en el pecho que le siguió,** vino el **segundo golpe con el mismo objeto,** pero **esta vez en su sien.** La derribó al piso, tras lo cual intentó defenderse con sus brazos y piernas, pero vino el tercer y cuarto golpe.

Stephen: ¿Esos fueron los que la mataron?

Lauren: No, siguió viva. El victimario **cambió el objeto contundente por una navaja corta,** y **la apuñaló cinco veces: una vez en el abdomen a la altura del páncreas,** otro en el **brazo izquierdo, entre bíceps y tríceps,** y las **otras tres en la garganta. Cortó su vena yugular, haciendo que se desangrara** en momentos. Fue una **muerte dolorosa y desesperante** para la joven.

Stephen: ¿No crees que le dio chance de gritar en algún momento mientras se desangraba? Tenemos evidencias de que alguien pudo observar el crimen mientras se llevaba a cabo, y creemos que fue porque escuchó algo.

Lauren: Es poco probable, pero eso se lo dejo a ustedes, los especialistas. De nuevo insisto, la víctima conocía a su asesino; **ni siquiera opuso tanta resistencia** a su muerte cuando él cambió su arma por la navaja.

Stephen: Sí. En su mirada se puede ver cómo está rogándole a su asesino que le de piedad. Lo que puedo prometerte, Lauren, es que vamos a capturar al desgraciado que está involucrado en esto. Así tenga que buscar bajo las piedras, voy a capturarlo.

Lauren: Es bueno saberlo. No ha sido fácil para mí, especialmente porque era tan joven y linda como mi hija. Suerte, de todas formas. El resto de los detalles están en este reporte. Puedes analizarlo para que veas lo que falta.

Stephen: Los tomaré en cuenta. Gracias por tu asistencia. Estaré regresando en unos días para informarte sobre la captura y confirmar si nuestra teoría fue correcta.

Lauren: Gracias, Stephen. Suerte.

English

Stephen: What's up, Lauren?

Lauren: Everything's okay, Stephen. I **guess you're here for that murder case in the back alley in Queens**, right?

Stephen: Exactly. I wanted to know **what kind of progress you've made with the body of the victim**. I don't want to give many details, but I've received slightly strange information. I **want to verify what I know with what you've observed**.

Lauren: Yes, I understand. Nothing is what it seems, and sometimes this type of case can end up surprising us, no? Well, **let's begin with my analysis**, so we can see if there's any type of relation with your discoveries.

Stephen: Perfect, I'm going to start taking note(s) while you speak. I'll surely have questions, so prepare yourself.

Lauren: Okay. Right, the victim was walking alone at that time, approximately at three-fifteen in the morning, apparently coming from a party. I know this because **she had alcohol in her blood, as well as a full bladder**.

Stephen: So you think she was in a place where she couldn't go to the bathroom, right? Good catch.

Lauren: Exactly. She probably decided to take a shortcut, which made her walk down the alley where she would meet her death.

Stephen: Yes, I agree that that's more or less how it went.

Lauren: She walked a few feet, but something made her stop. **Her body wasn't in motion when she received her first blow. It was a descending blow on her shoulder with a blunt metal object**. I think **they aimed at her skull**, but she was able to dodge the attack very slightly. It wasn't enough to knock her to the ground, but even then she didn't try to escape.

Stephen: She didn't attempt to flee?

Lauren: No. In fact, I have a theory about that.

Stephen: Well, I have one too. She knew her aggressor.

Lauren: Exactly! After receiving **her first blow and the shove in the chest that followed**, the **second blow followed with the same object**, but **this time in her temple**. It knocked her to the ground, after which she tried to defend herself with arms and legs, but the third and fourth blows followed.

Stephen: Were those the ones that killed her?

Lauren: No, she was still alive. The aggressor **swapped the blunt object for a short knife**, and **he stabbed her five times**: once in the abdomen around her pancreas, another in her left arm, between biceps and triceps, and the other three times in her throat. He **sliced the jugular vein, causing her to bleed to death** in moments. It was a **painful and desperate death** for the young lady.

Stephen: Don't you think she got a chance to scream at one point as she bled out? We have evidence that somebody may have observed the crime while it was taking place, and we think it is because they heard something.

Lauren: It's very unlikely, but I leave that to you guys, the specialists. Again, I insist, the victim knew her aggressor; **she didn't even show much resistance** to her death when he'd traded his weapon for a knife.

Stephen: Yeah. In her eyes you can see how she was begging her murderer for mercy. What I can promise you, Lauren, is that we're going to capture the bastard that is involved in this. Even if I have to leave no stone unturned, I'm going to capture him.

Lauren: That's good to know. It hasn't been easy for me, especially because she was so young and pretty like my daughter. Good luck, anyway. The rest of the details are right here in this report. You can analyze this so you can see what's missing.

Stephen: I'll take that all into account. Thanks for your assistance. I'll be returning in some days to inform you about the capture and confirm if our theory was right.

Lauren: Thanks Stephen, good luck.

CHAPTER 24

IMAGINARY ILLNESS
TODO ESTÁ EN TU CABEZA —
IT'S ALL IN YOUR HEAD

Vocabulary List

- **Creo que es algo serio que podría ameritar observación médica** = I think it's something serious that could require medical observation

- **Las últimas dos veces pudimos descartar que tuvieras alguna enfermedad** = The last two times we were able to rule out any sickness

- **¿No será que de nuevo estás sufriendo de tu hipocondría?** = Might it just be you suffering from your hypochondria again?

- **Esta vez si me siento muy mal** = This time I do feel really bad

- **Tengo dos meses con un dolor de cabeza, y estoy viendo borroso** = I've been suffering from a headache for two months, and my vision is blurry

- **Me duele el estómago muy seguido** = My stomach hurts very often

- **Creo que tengo cáncer** = I think I have cancer

- **Vamos a ver tus resultados** = Let's look at your results

- **Muchos tipos de cáncer se comienzan a manifestar con esos síntomas** = Many types of cancer start to manifest with those symptoms

- **El dolor de cabeza pudieran ser tumores cerebrales** = The headache could be brain tumors

- **Tienes la hemoglobina un poco baja** = You have a slightly low hemoglobin count

- **Síntomas preocupantes** = Worrying symptoms
- **No hay señal de tumores** = There are no signs of tumors
- **Abre los ojos** = Open your eyes
- **Sigue la linterna con tu mirada** = Follow the flashlight with your eyes
- **Deberías tomarme la tensión** = You should measure my blood pressure
- **¿Tengo la temperatura corporal alta?** = Is my bodily temperature too high?
- **Déjame revisar ahora tus oídos y garganta** = Let me check your ears and throat now
- **Sufres de una condición** = You suffer from a condition
- **Se manifiesta como el temor irracional a sufrir una enfermedad grave** = It manifests as an irrational fear of suffering a serious illness
- **Sólo necesitas lentes** = You only need glasses
- **Puede que estés sufriendo de acidez, o gastritis** = You could simply be suffering from heartburn, or gastritis
- **Tienes síntomas de esta última enfermedad** = You have symptoms of this latter illness
- **Bastante descanso** = A lot of rest

Gus: Finalmente, doctora. Realmente necesitaba verla, porque me he sentido muy mal estos últimos meses, y **creo que es algo serio que podría ameritar observación médica.**

Cindy: Hola de nuevo, Gus. Tenías tiempo sin venir, recuerdo que **las últimas dos veces pudimos descartar que tuvieras alguna enfermedad.** De antemano te pregunto, **¿no será que de nuevo estás sufriendo de tu hipocondría?**

Gus: Eso no es justo conmigo, doctora, **esta vez si me siento muy mal. Tengo dos meses con un dolor de cabeza, y estoy viendo borroso.** Además, **me duele el estómago muy seguido. Creo que tengo cáncer.**

Cindy: Bueno, decir que tienes cáncer así de buenas a primeras es un poco prematuro. **Vamos a ver tus resultados.** ¿Los trajiste contigo?

Gus: Claro, claro... Aquí están. Estuve leyendo en internet, y **muchos tipos de cáncer se comienzan a manifestar con esos síntomas.** El de estómago, por ejemplo. Y **el dolor de cabeza pudieran ser tumores cerebrales.**

Cindy: Bueno, acá dice que **tienes la hemoglobina un poco baja.** Del resto pareces no estar presentando **síntomas preocupantes.** Tus exámenes de heces y orina salieron bien.

Gus: ¿Viste? Tengo la hemoglobina baja. Eso es una muy importante señal. Seguramente ya mi cuerpo se está adaptando a los tumores.

Cindy: Gus, por favor, debes calmarte y dejar que yo haga mi trabajo. **No hay señal de tumores.** Vamos a ver qué tal estás. **Abre los ojos,** voy a mirar con mi linterna. **Sigue la linterna con tu mirada,** por favor.

Gus: Deberías tomarme la tensión apenas termines. Bueno, ya estoy siguiendo la linterna. ¿Ves mis ojos haciendo señales extrañas? **¿Tengo la temperatura corporal alta?**

Cindy: No, Gus. Estás bien. **Déjame revisar ahora tus oídos y garganta.** Abre bien la boca y di *ahhh.*

Gus: Ahhh... Me observó algún tipo de problema ahí, ¿cierto?

Cindy: No, Gus, tampoco observé nada. ¿Qué esperas que encuentre? ¿Hay alguien en tu familia que haya sufrido de cáncer?

Gus: Pues no, pero eso—

Cindy: ¿Has estado comiendo bien? ¿Tienes actividad física?

Gus: Sí, creo que ambas cosas. O así me parece, al menos.

Cindy: Entonces no tienes nada de qué preocuparte. Hay personas que cumplen con todas las señales preocupantes, pero no es tu caso. Deberías tranquilizarte y vivir tu vida, estás angustiándote innecesariamente con esto de pensar que estás enfermo de gravedad.

Gus: ¿Realmente piensas eso? Siempre he tenido mucho miedo de caer enfermo y no tener quien me cuide, de estar sufriendo por mi salud y no tener cómo pagar el tratamiento. No es fácil.

Cindy: Sé que no es fácil, pero tampoco te la pones fácil. **Sufres de una condición**; eres hipocondríaco. **Se manifiesta como el temor irracional a sufrir una enfermedad grave**, además de vincular todos los síntomas con una de estas condiciones. Creer que sufres de cáncer por dolores de cabeza es algo exagerado, Gus. Al parecer **sólo necesitas lentes**.

Gus: ¿Lentes? ¿Cómo puedes estar tan segura de eso?

Cindy: Porque lo noté al revisar tus ojos.

Gus: ¿Y qué tal lo del estómago? ¿Cómo se explica eso? Porque de verdad que ha sido un dolor persistente.

Cindy: Simplemente **puede que estés sufriendo de acidez, o gastritis. Tienes síntomas de esta última enfermedad**, así que no me sorprendería. No siempre tiene por qué ser algo grave, Gus.

Gus: ¿Así que yo he estado preocupándome en vano? No puede ser...

Cindy: Sí, porque al final del día lo que necesitas es **bastante descanso** y quizás algún medicamento para calmar tus nervios. Ah, y algo para la gastritis. Ahí estarás como nuevo.

Gus: ¿Estás segura? Eso sería muy bueno para ser verdad, si te soy sincero.

Cindy: Sí, estoy bastante segura. Todo va a mejorar pronto, pero debes dejar de preocuparte en exceso. Por favor, hazlo por tu salud.

Gus: ¿Sabes qué? Lo voy a hacer. Tienes toda la razón. Voy a dejar de pensar en eso. ¡Gracias doctora!

English

Gus: Finally, doc. I really needed to see you, because I've felt really bad these past months, and **I think it's something serious that could require medical observation**.

Cindy: Hello again, Gus. You haven't come for a long time, I remember that **the last two times we were able to rule out any sickness**. Just before we start I'm going to ask, **might it just be you suffering from hypochondria again?**

Gus: That's not fair doctor, **this time I do feel really bad. I've been suffering from a headache for two months, and my vision is blurry**. Furthermore, **my stomach hurts very often. I think I have cancer**.

Cindy: Well, saying that you have cancer just like that is a bit premature. **Let's look at your results**. Did you bring them with you?

Gus: Sure, sure... They're right here. I was reading on the internet, and **many types of cancer start to manifest with those symptoms**. Stomach cancer, for example. And **the headache could be brain tumors**.

Cindy: Okay, it says here that **you have a slightly low hemoglobin count**. Otherwise, you don't seem to show any **worrying symptoms**. Your stool and urine exams show great results.

Gus: See? I have low hemoglobin. That's a very important sign. Surely my body is already adapting to the tumors.

Cindy: Gus, please, you should calm down and allow me to do my work. **There are no signs of tumors**. Let's see how you're doing. **Open your eyes**; I'm going to look at them with my flashlight. **Follow the flashlight with your eyes**, please.

Gus: You should measure my blood pressure once you're done. All right, I'm following the torch now. See my eyes doing strange signals? **Is my bodily temperature too high?**

Cindy: No, Gus. You're okay. **Let me check your ears and throat now.** Open your mouth wide and say *ahhh*.

Gus: Ahhh... You saw some type of problems there, didn't you?

Cindy: No, Gus, I didn't observe anything there either. What do you expect me to find? Is there anyone in your family who has suffered from cancer?

Gus: Well, no, but that—

Cindy: Have you been eating well? Do you partake in physical activity?

Gus: Yes, I believe I do both things. Or so it seems, at least.

Cindy: Then you have nothing to worry about. There are people who check all of the worrying boxes, but that isn't your case. You should relax and live your life; you're worrying yourself unnecessarily thinking you're sick, dying.

Gus: Do you really think that? I've always been very afraid of falling sick and not having anyone to take care of me, of suffering from health issues and not having the money to pay for the treatment. It isn't easy.

Cindy: I know it's not, but you're not making it easy for yourself either. **You suffer from a condition**; you're a hypochondriac. **It manifests as an irrational fear of suffering a serious illness**, as well as linking all of your symptoms to one of these conditions. To think you suffer from cancer because of a few headaches is somewhat exaggerated, Gus. It seems **you only need glasses**.

Gus: Glasses? How can you be so sure of that?

Cindy: Because I realized it when I studied your eyes.

Gus: What about the problem with my stomach? How do you explain that? Because it really has been a persistent pain.

Cindy: You could simply be suffering from heartburn, or gastritis. You have symptoms of this latter illness, so it wouldn't surprise me. It doesn't always have to be something serious, Gus.

Gus: So I've been worrying in vain? That cannot be...

Cindy: Yes, because at the end of the day what you need is **a lot of rest** and maybe some medication to calm those nerves. Ah, and something for your gastritis. You'll be like a new man after that.

Gus: Are you sure? That would be too good to be true, if I'm being honest.

Cindy: Yes, I'm absolutely sure. Everything will get better soon, but you have to stop worrying excessively. Please, do it for your health.

Gus: You know what? I'll do it. You're completely right. I'll stop thinking of that. Thanks doctor!

CHAPTER 25

DEATH OF A LOVED ONE
ESTO NO SERÁ FÁCIL DE ESCUCHAR — THIS WON'T BE EASY TO HEAR

Vocabulary List

- **¿Qué sucedió anoche? ¿Cómo sigue mi padre?** = What happened last night? How is my father?
- **¿Son malas noticias?** = Is there bad news?
- **¡No me diga que le pasó algo a mi papá!** = Don't tell me something happened to my dad!
- **Tu papá falleció anoche** = Your father passed away last night
- **Su corazón no aguantó más, y tuvo un paro respiratorio** = His heart couldn't resist anymore, and he went into respiratory arrest
- **Había recibido terapia de radiación por mucho tiempo** = His body had been receiving radiation therapy for too long
- **Estaba muy deteriorado** = He was very worn
- **Su corazón ya no tenía la misma fuerza** = His heart didn't have the same strength
- **Su cáncer estaba en una etapa sumamente avanzada** = His cancer was in an extremely advanced stage
- **Luchó todo lo que pudo** = He fought all he could
- **Esa etapa de cáncer puede vencer a cualquiera** = That stage of cancer can beat anybody
- **¡Yo lo vi ayer y estaba fuerte!** = I saw him yesterday and he looked strong!
- **Sentía como su vida se le escapaba entre los dedos** = He felt his life slipping through his fingers

177

- **Yo mismo vi cómo se apagó la luz en sus ojos** = I myself saw how the light went out in his eyes
- **Perder a un ser querido jamás es fácil** = Losing a loved one is never easy
- **En un accidente de tránsito** = In a car accident
- **El cáncer de tu papá al parecer era de carácter genético** = Your dad's cancer was apparently one of genetic character
- **Su cáncer estaba en una fase casi terminal** = His cancer was already in an almost terminal state
- **Subestimó su enfermedad** = He underestimated his illness
- **Ánimo y fuerza** = Strength and belief

Rose: Hola doctor, vine tan rápido como pude. Recibí la llamada de su secretaria diciéndome que quería hablar conmigo. **¿Qué sucedió anoche? ¿Cómo sigue mi padre?**

Walter: Hola Rose. Quiero que tomes asiento, ya que necesitamos hablar mejor de los últimos acontecimientos.

Rose: ¿Son malas noticias? Su cara me lo dice todo, **¡no me diga que le pasó algo a mi papá!**

Walter: Vamos, Rose. Necesito que estés sentada y calmada antes de que podamos hablar bien.

Rose: ¡Oh, Dios mío! Ya me senté - ¡ahora sólo dígame qué pasó!

Walter: Rose, lamento decírtelo... **Tu papá falleció anoche** a las dos y treinta y cinco de la mañana. **Su corazón no aguantó más, y tuvo un paro respiratorio**. Tratamos de ponernos en contacto contigo en seguida, pero no fue hasta ahora que pudimos localizarte.

Rose: ¡No! ¡Esto es terrible! Lo vi ayer y... ¡Estaba bien, doctor! ¿Cómo pudo morir si estaba bien? ¡¿Cómo?!

Walter: Su cuerpo **había recibido terapia de radiación por mucho tiempo. Estaba muy deteriorado**, y **su corazón ya no tenía la misma fuerza. Su cáncer estaba en una etapa sumamente avanzada**. Hicimos todo lo que pudimos.

Rose: ¿Está seguro de eso? Yo creo que debí llevarlo a otro hospital, aun estaba fuerte y podía durarnos unos meses más.

Walter: Decir eso es injusto con tu padre, Rose. Él **luchó todo lo que pudo**, y se sentía feliz acá bajo nuestro trato. Pero se nos fue, y era algo que todos sabíamos que podía pasar. Era un gran hombre, pero **esa etapa de cáncer puede vencer a cualquiera**.

Rose: ¡Yo lo vi ayer y estaba fuerte! ¿Cómo me explica eso, doctor? No quiero que suene como que no les agradezco todo lo que hicieron, de verdad, pero siento que estaba bien...

Walter: Tu padre hizo lo que pudo para mantenerse fuerte delante de ti y tus hermanos, pero realmente estaba muy mal. Me confesó varias veces que **sentía como su vida se le escapaba entre los dedos**.

Rose: ¿Habló con usted? ¿Qué más le dijo? Si hay algo importante, debo saberlo ya.

Walter: Me pidió que supiera calmarte, y que no dejara que dijeras algo cruel. Sabía que estarías muy dolida, pero se despidió con una sonrisa. **Yo mismo vi cómo se apagó la luz en sus ojos**. Se veía en paz.

Rose: Oh, doctor...

Walter: Entiendo tu dolor, Rose. **Perder a un ser querido jamás es fácil**, y perderlo de esta manera es mucho más difícil, más duro que cualquier otra manera. Yo sé lo que es eso – yo también perdí mi papá hace años.

Rose: ¿Sí? ¿Cómo lo perdió?

Walter: En un accidente de tránsito. Yo apenas tenía dieciséis años.

Rose: Entiendo. Que lamentable. En mi caso quisiera entender, ¿sabes? ¿Por qué le pasó esto a mi papá? ¿Por qué él? Comía bien, hacía ejercicios, y nunca tenía malas intenciones.

Walter: El cáncer de tu papá al parecer era de carácter genético. Sus padres ambos sufrieron de ese mismo cáncer; esperemos que no le toque a más nadie de la familia.

Rose: Eso también lo espero. No podría resistir esto una vez más.

Walter: Igual tenemos que empezar a hacer pruebas a los integrantes de la familia pronto, aunque sea para descartar. Tu papá esperó mucho para venir a verme, ya **su cáncer estaba en una fase casi terminal**. En otras circunstancias quizás hubiésemos podido salvarlo.

Rose: Sí, eso lo recuerdo bien. **Subestimó su enfermedad**, y quizás por eso es que ya no está con nosotros.

Walter: ¿Ahora qué sucederá? ¿Ya tenían preparado su testamento?

Rose: Sí, ya tenemos el papeleo hecho. Veamos qué sucede. Muchas gracias por esta conversación, doctor. Lo necesitaba. Voy a tomarme un momento a solas, si no le molesta.

Walter: Está bien, Rose. Hablamos cuando te sientas cómoda; así me indicas qué se hará con su cuerpo. **Ánimo y fuerza**.

Rose: Gracias, Doctor Walter.

English

Rose: Hello doctor, I came as quickly as I could. I received the call from your secretary asking me to come and talk with you. **What happened last night? How is my father?**

Walter: Hello Rose. I want you to take a seat, because we need to talk a bit more about the latest events.

Rose: Is there bad news? Your face says it all, **don't tell me something happened to my dad!**

Walter: Come on, Rose. I need you to be sitting and calmed down before we can speak properly. What I'm about to tell you isn't easy.

Rose: Oh my God! I'm sitting now – just tell me what happened!

Walter: Rose, I'm sorry to say this... **Your father passed away last night** at two-thirty-five in the morning. **His heart couldn't resist anymore, and he went into respiratory arrest.** We tried to make contact with you right away, but it wasn't until now that we managed to locate you.

Rose: No! That is terrible! I saw him yesterday and... He was okay, doctor! How could he die if he was okay? How?!

Walter: His body had been receiving radiation therapy for too long. He was very worn, and **his heart didn't have the same strength** anymore. **His cancer was in an extremely advanced stage.** We did what we could.

Rose: Are you sure about that? I think I should have taken him to another hospital, since he was strong and could have survived for another few months.

Walter: Saying that is unfair with your father, Rose. **He fought all he could,** and he felt happy here in our care. Nevertheless, he's gone, and it was something that everyone knew could happen. He was a great man, but **that stage of cancer can beat anybody.**

Rose: I saw him yesterday and he looked strong! How can you explain that, doctor? I don't want it to sound as if I'm not grateful for everything you've done, but I really feel that he was fine...

Walter: Your father did what he could to keep himself strong in front of you and your siblings, but he really wasn't well. He confessed to me several times that **he felt his life slipping through his fingers**.

Rose: Did he speak with you? What else did he say? If there's anything important, I have to know now.

Walter: He asked me to find a way to calm you down, and not allow you to say something cruel. He told me he knew you'd be very hurt, but he said goodbye with a smile. **I myself saw how the light went out in his eyes**. He seemed to be in peace.

Rose: Oh, doctor...

Walter: I understand your pain, Rose. **Losing a loved one is never easy**, and losing one in this way is much more difficult, more difficult than in any other way. I know what this is like – I also lost my father some years ago.

Rose: Yes? How did you lose him?

Walter: **In a car accident**. I was only sixteen years old.

Rose: I understand. How unfortunate. In my case I would like to understand, you know? Why did this happen to my dad? Why him? He ate well, exercised, and he never had bad intentions.

Walter: **Your dad's cancer was apparently one of genetic character**. Both of his parents suffered from that same cancer; we hope it doesn't pass on to anybody else in the family.

Rose: I hope that too. I don't think I could handle this another time.

Walter: We still have to start doing our testing on other members of the family soon, even if it is just to rule out. Your father waited too long to come and see me; **his cancer was already in an almost terminal state**. In other circumstances we may have been able to save him.

Rose: Yes, I remember that well. **He underestimated his illness**, and that may just be why he isn't with us anymore.

Walter: Now what will happen? Did you have his will ready?

Rose: Yes, we have the paperwork done. Let's see what happens. Thanks a lot for this conversation, doctor. I needed it. I'm going to take some time off on my own, if there's no problem with you.

Walter: It's okay, Rose. We can talk when you feel comfortable; that way you can indicate what we'll do with the body. **Strength and belief**.

Rose: Thanks, Doctor Walter.

CHAPTER 26

REANIMATION

¿CUÁNTOS DEDOS TENGO ACÁ? — HOW MANY FINGERS DO I HAVE HERE?

Vocabulary List

- **¿Por qué me duele tanto la cabeza?** = Why does my head hurt so much?
- **Recibiste un fuerte golpe en la cabeza; te dejó inconsciente por varios minutos** = You took quite a blow to the head; it knocked you cold for several moments
- **Estamos en una ambulancia** = We're inside an ambulance
- **El golpe te lastimó el cráneo** = The blow hurt your brain
- **Estás sangrando** = You're bleeding
- **¿Eres doctora o algo así?** = Are you a doctor or something like that?
- **Soy paramédico** = I'm a paramedic
- **Llegué a la escena poco después de que tuviste el accidente en motocicleta** = I arrived to the scene shortly after you had the motorcycle accident
- **Su moto dio varios giros y él se lastimó** = His bike spun several times and he got really hurt
- **¿Está muerto?** = Is he dead?
- **Trata de enfocar tu vista en él** = Try to focus your vision on it
- **Estoy muy mareado** = I'm very dizzy
- **Habíamos consumido bastante alcohol antes de grabar** = We had consumed a lot of alcohol before filming
- **Estás muy desorientado, lo sé** = You're very disoriented, I know

- **No es sencillo regresar a la normalidad tras un golpe de ese tipo** = It's not easy to return to normal after a blow of that magnitude
- **Fue llevado de emergencia a cuidados intensivos** = He was taken to emergency intensive care
- **¿Ya has sufrido accidentes por conducir ebrio?** = So you've already suffered accidents while driving under the influence?
- **¿Ya tienes mejor orientación de la situación, Andrew?** = Do you have better orientation of your surroundings, Andrew?
- **¿Crees que estaré bien?** = Do you think I'll be okay?
- **Pronto serás trasladado a emergencia para que hagan el resto** = Soon you'll be taken to emergency so they can do the rest

Spanish

Allison: ¿Hola? ¿Estás bien? Vamos, responde. Bien, ahí estamos.

Andrew: Uhh… ¿hola? ¿Quién eres tú? ¿Qué sucede? **¿Por qué me duele tanto la cabeza?**

Allison: Recibiste un fuerte golpe en la cabeza; te dejó inconsciente por varios minutos. No me sorprendería si no tienes idea de lo que está ocurriendo ahora mismo.

Andrew: ¡¿Qué?! ¡¿Un golpe?! ¿Cómo? Ni siquiera noté lo que está ocurriendo.

Allison: ¿Y qué está ocurriendo según lo que ves? ¿Sabes en dónde estás?

Andrew: Creo que me están llevando a casa o algo. ¿Estamos en un vehículo, cierto? Estuve tomando mucho.

Allison: Estamos en una ambulancia, Andrew. Vamos hacia el hospital. **El golpe te lastimó el cráneo. Estás sangrando.**

Andrew: ¿Es en serio? ¿Andrew? Cierto, ese es mi nombre. **¿Eres doctora o algo así?**

Allison: Sí, algo así. **Soy paramédico,** y **llegué a la escena poco después de que tuviste el accidente en motocicleta.**

Andrew: No entiendo, ¿qué me estás diciendo?

Allison: ¿Acaso no recuerdas lo que estabas haciendo antes de que te dieras el golpe?

Andrew: No, no recuerdo nada. Sólo recuerdo que… ¿viste a Jorge? ¿Jorge está bien?

Allison: ¿Tu compañero? Él no está nada bien. **Su moto dio varios giros y él se lastimó.**

Andrew: No puede ser. **¿Está muerto?** Vaya, no veo nada bien. Siento que el mundo me da muchas vueltas. En serio no debí tomar y conducir.

Allison: Mira mi dedo. Sigue mi dedo con tus ojos. **Trata de enfocar tu vista en él.** ¿Puedes hacerlo?

Andrew: Sí, supongo. **Estoy muy mareado.**

Allison: Háblame de ti, Andrew. ¿Quién eres? ¿A qué te dedicas? Todo esto te ayudará a regresar a la normalidad.

Andrew: Bueno, mi nombre es Andrew y soy deportista extremo; me encantan las motocicletas y quizás es por eso que estoy acá en esta ambulancia. Trataba de realizar un video corto con mi amigo Jorge, pero por lo visto algo salió mal. **Habíamos consumido bastante alcohol antes de grabar.**

Allison: Interesante. ¿Qué iban a hacer con el video? ¿Planeaban que lo viera algún estudio de televisión?

Andrew: No, era para subirla a nuestro canal en las redes. Creo que se debe haber dañado la cámara, así que ya no importa. ¿Vamos al hospital, no?

Allison: Sí, a eso vamos. **Estás muy desorientado, lo sé. No es sencillo regresar a la normalidad tras un golpe de ese tipo.**

Andrew: No, para nada. Casi no puedo recordar quién soy. ¿Qué me dijiste de Jorge?

Allison: Fue llevado de emergencia a cuidados intensivos. No está nada bien. Pero por ahora no te preocupes por él, sino por ti mismo. ¿Puedes respirar con normalidad?

Andrew: Sí, estoy seguro que sí. Creo que mi esposa estará algo angustiada cuando sepa que tuve un accidente. No es primera vez que me pasa algo así, pero esta vez fue mucho peor que la anterior.

Allison: ¿La vez anterior? ¿Así que **ya has sufrido accidentes por conducir ebrio?**

Andrew: No debí decir eso. Olvídalo, doctora. No es importante en este momento, es algo que dije por decir.

Allison: No, Andrew. Sí es importante. Debes tener mucho cuidado. Podrías no sólo matarte tú, sino matar a otras personas en la carretera. Imagínate ser el papá de alguien y que te llamen para avisar que esa persona murió por un conductor ebrio. ¿Cómo te sentirías?

Andrew: Furioso... desesperado... Tienes razón, entiendo tu punto. Y ahora soy yo el que está lastimado. Y Jorge...

Allison: Exacto, Jorge está mucho peor. Por eso mismo debes ordenar tu vida y tomar las decisiones correctas. Ya has tenido dos accidentes; no creo que tengas otro chance igual. **¿Ya tienes mejor orientación de la situación, Andrew?**

Andrew: Algo así. Estoy comenzando a entender más lo que ocurre. *¿Crees que estaré bien?*

Allison: Sí creo. Especialmente si tomas la decisión de arreglar tu vida. Sé que puedes hacerlo. Ya estamos entrando al hospital; **pronto serás trasladado a emergencia para que hagan el resto**.

Andrew: Excelente. Gracias por tus consejos.

Allison: Espero los apliques. Ahora ve, mucha suerte con el resto.

Andrew: ¡Igualmente!

English

Allison: Hello? Are you okay? Come on, respond. Yeah, that's it.

Andrew: Uhh… hello? Who are you? What's going on? **Why does my head hurt so much?**

Allison: You took quite a blow to the head; it knocked you cold for several moments. I wouldn't be surprised if you don't know what's happening right now.

Andrew: What?! A blow?! How? I didn't even realize what was happening.

Allison: And what is happening according to what you see? Do you know where you are?

Andrew: I think I'm being taken home or something. We're in a vehicle, aren't we? I had a lot to drink.

Allison: We're inside an ambulance, Andrew. We're headed towards the hospital. **The blow hurt your brain. You're bleeding.**

Andrew: Are you serious? Andrew? Right, that's my name. **Are you a doctor or something like that?**

Allison: Yeah, something like that. **I'm a paramedic**, and **I arrived at the scene shortly after you had the motorcycle accident.**

Andrew: I don't understand, what are you telling me?

Allison: Don't you even remember what you were doing before the impact?

Andrew: No, I don't remember anything. All I can remember is… did you see Jorge? Is Jorge okay?

Allison: Your partner? He's not in good shape at all. **His bike spun several times and he got really hurt.**

Andrew: It can't be. **Is he dead?** Wow, I can't even see properly or anything. I feel like the whole world is spinning around me. I really shouldn't have drunk and drove.

Allison: Look at my finger. Follow the finger with your eyes. **Try to focus**

your vision on it. Can you do it?

Andrew: Yes, I guess. **I'm very dizzy**.

Allison: Tell me about yourself, Andrew. Who are you? What do you do for a living? All of these questions will help you return to normal.

Andrew: Well, my name is Andrew, and I'm an extreme sports enthusiast; I love motorcycles, and that's probably why I'm lying here in this ambulance. I was trying to film a short video with my friend Jorge, but it seems that something went wrong. **We had consumed a lot of alcohol before filming**.

Allison: Interesting. What were you going to do with the video? Were you planning on having a television studio watch it?

Andrew: No, it was just for us to upload on our networks. I think the camera may have been damaged, so it doesn't matter anymore. We're on the way to the hospital, right?

Allison: Yes, that's where we're headed. **You're very disoriented, I know. It's not easy to return to normal after a blow of that magnitude**.

Andrew: No, not at all. I can barely remember who I am. What did you say about Jorge?

Allison: He was taken to emergency intensive care. He doesn't look well at all. However, for now don't worry about him, only about yourself. Can you breathe normally?

Andrew: Yeah, I'm sure I can. I think my wife is going to be somewhat distressed when she finds out I had an accident. It's not the first time something like this happens, but this time was much worse than the last.

Allison: The last time? **So you've already suffered accidents while driving under the influence?**

Andrew: I shouldn't have said that. Forget it, doctor. It's not important right now, only something I said out of the blue.

Allison: No, Andrew. It is important. You have to be very careful. You could not only kill yourself, but also kill someone else on the road. Imagine being somebody's father and receiving a call telling you that a drunk driver killed them. How would you feel?

Andrew: Furious... desperate... You're right, I understand your point.

Now I'm the one that's hurt. And Jorge...

Allison: Exactly, Jorge is much worse off. That's exactly why you have to organize your life and make the right decisions. You've already had two accidents; I don't think you'll have another opportunity. **Do you have better orientation of your surroundings, Andrew?**

Andrew: Something like that. I'm starting to better understand what's going on. **Do you think I'll be okay?**

Allison: Yes, I think. Especially if you make the decision of fixing your life. I know you can do it. We're entering the hospital; **soon you'll be taken to emergency so they can do the rest**.

Andrew: Excellent. Thanks for your advice.

Allison: I hope you make good use of it. Now go, good luck with the rest.

Andrew: Same!

CHAPTER 27

SHOCKING DISCOVERY

¡TENEMOS QUE OPERARTE YA MISMO! — WE'RE GOING TO HAVE TO OPERATE YOU NOW!

Vocabulary List

- **He tenido mucho dolor últimamente, y tengo diarrea constante** = I've had a lot of pain lately, and I have constant diarrhea

- **¿Aplicaste la dieta que te receté?** = Did you apply the diet I prescribed?

- **Recuerdo que estabas comiendo muy mal** = I remember you weren't eating properly

- **De verdad que no hallo qué medicina tomar para el dolor** = I really can't find a medicine to take for the pain

- **Vamos a ver qué sucede acá con una ecografía abdominal** = Let's see what's happening here with an abdominal ultrasound

- **Respira profundo y no pongas tensos los músculos del abdomen** = Breathe deeply and don't make your abdominal muscles tense

- **Descríbeme el tipo de dolor que has sufrido, por favor** = Describe the type of pain you've been feeling, please

- **Comenzó como un leve dolor en el medio de mi abdomen, el cual fue pasando al lado superior derecho** = It started as a light pain in the middle of my abdomen, which then moved towards the top right side

- **Empeoró en los últimos dos días** = It worsened in the last two day

- **Incrementaba a su máximo después de comer** = Grew to its peak after I ate
- **Náuseas, vómitos al menos dos veces al día, dolor en el pecho** = Nausea, vomiting at least twice a day, chest pains
- **También he tenido exceso de gases** = I've also had an excess of gas
- **¿Y has tenido fiebre?** = And have you had a fever?
- **Inhala profundo** = Breathe deeply
- **Tu dolor se ha debido a la grave formación de cálculos biliares** = Your pain can be due to the serious formation of gallbladder stones
- **Voy a remitirte a cirugía para hoy mismo o mañana** = I am going to schedule a surgery for today or tomorrow
- **Son como los cálculos renales, pero estos no se forman en los riñones sino en la vesícula** = They are like kidney stones, but these are formed in the gallbladder
- **No es hasta que éstas comienzan a cristalizarse en masa y obstruir los ductos que empiezan los problemas** = It isn't until these begin to crystallize in mass and obstruct the ducts that the problems begin
- **Ya comienzas a tener obstrucción** = You're already starting to have obstruction
- **Vas a necesitar reposo y una dieta con cero grasas** = You'll need complete rest and a no-fat diet

Spanish

Jamie: A ver, Skyler, ¿qué te trae a la clínica el día de hoy? ¿Otra vez con tus problemas de estómago?

Skyler: Sí, **he tenido mucho dolor últimamente, y tengo diarrea constante.**

Jamie: ¿Aplicaste la dieta que te receté? Recuerdo que estabas comiendo muy mal. Sólo comías comida rápida, y tomabas muchas bebidas carbonatadas.

Skyler: Sí, hice todo lo que me dijiste, pero no está haciendo efecto. **De verdad que no hallo qué medicina tomar para el dolor**; es insoportable y me está arruinando mi rutina.

Jamie: Vamos a ver qué sucede acá con una ecografía abdominal. Seguramente sabremos lo que ocurre.

Skyler: Sí, por favor. Me urge saber. Ya es demasiado; siento que no voy a poder seguir mi semestre en la universidad si este problema continúa.

Jamie: Ya vas a sentirte mejor, Skyler. Ánimo. Súbete la camiseta un poco y acuéstate acá. Vas a sentir algo frío mientras te lubrico el abdomen para la revisión.

Skyler: Ok, no hay problema. Sí, está bastante frío. ¿Esto va a ayudar a saber qué ocurre?

Jamie: Sí. Ahora, **respira profundo y no pongas tensos los músculos del abdomen.** Esto va a ser breve, pero necesito poder ver lo que está pasando allí adentro. **Descríbeme el tipo de dolor que has sufrido, por favor.**

Skyler: Bueno, **comenzó como un leve dolor en el medio de mi abdomen, el cual fue pasando al lado superior derecho. Empeoró en los últimos dos días, e incrementaba a su máximo después de comer.**

Jamie: ¿Algún otro síntoma?

Skyler: Náuseas, vómitos al menos dos veces al día, dolor en el pecho... También he tenido exceso de gases, más de lo que he tenido jamás.

Jamie: Entiendo. **¿Y has tenido fiebre?**

Skyler: Poca, pero sí. Esto ha sido terrible, y no me ha dejado estudiar para mis exámenes.

Jamie: De acuerdo. **Inhala profundo**... ahora exhala. Inhala de nuevo... exhala de nuevo. Ah, creo que veo algo.

Skyler: ¿Qué estás viendo? ¿Qué ocurre, doctor?

Jamie: Un momento, Skyler. Estoy viendo algo que puede ser la causa. Ya, creo que sé qué está ocurriendo. Esto no está bien.

Skyler: Me está asustando, doctor. Por favor, dígame qué ocurre.

Jamie: De acuerdo. Arregla tu camiseta y siéntate acá. Debemos movernos rápido. Esto va a requerir una intervención de emergencia. Nada demasiado serio, pero hay que extraer eso.

Skyler: ¿Qué tengo? ¿Qué está ocurriendo?

Jamie: Bueno, resulta que **tu dolor se ha debido a la grave formación de cálculos biliares**, los cuales te están haciendo mucho daño. Este problema va a continuar hasta que se extraiga, por lo que **voy a remitirte a cirugía para hoy mismo o mañana**. No puede pasar de mañana, porque podría convertirse en algo serio. Podría provocar la muerte.

Skyler: ¡No puede ser! ¡¿Cálculos biliares?!￼ Nunca he oído sobre eso, ¿de qué trata?

Jamie: Son como los cálculos renales, pero estos no se forman en los riñones sino en la vesícula. Uno puede pasar la vida entera con cierta cantidad y tamaño de piedras en la vesícula sin ningún síntoma, pero **no es hasta que éstas comienzan a cristalizarse en masa y obstruir los ductos que empiezan los problemas.** En tu caso particular, **ya comienzas a tener obstrucción.** Va a empeorar si no se te opera.

Skyler: Vaya, entiendo. Con razón me he sentido tan mal. ¿Entonces qué debo hacer para prepararme?

Jamie: Debes decirme primero cuándo te piensas operar. ¿Tienes disponibilidad hoy? Dentro de tres horas, más o menos.

Skyler: Sí, va a tener que ser hoy. Le diré a mi madre que me traiga ropa y una manta para dormir. ¿Cuánto tiempo tardaré recuperándome de la operación?

Jamie: Son aproximadamente unas semanas, en las que **vas a necesitar**

reposo y una dieta con cero grasas. ¿Estás dispuesta?

Skyler: Sí, mientras signifique que me voy a curar. Bueno, preparémonos para la intervención entonces.

Jamie: Vamos. Llamaré a la enfermera en seguida.

English

Jamie: Let's see, Skyler, what brings you to the clinic today? Are you having stomach problems again?

Skyler: Yes, **I've had a lot of pain lately, and I have constant diarrhea.**

Jamie: Did you apply the diet I prescribed? I remember you weren't eating properly. You only ate fast food, and drank carbonated drinks.

Skyler: Yes, I did everything that you told me to, but it isn't working on me. **I really can't find a medicine to take for the pain**; it's unbearable and it's ruining my routine.

Jamie: Let's see what's happening here with an abdominal ultrasound. It'll surely help us know what's going on.

Skyler: Yes, please. I really need to know. It's too much; I feel that I won't be able to continue my semester at university if this problem continues.

Jamie: You're going to be okay, Skyler. Be strong. Lift your shirt slightly and lie down here. You're going to feel something cold while I lubricate your abdomen for the examination.

Skyler: Ok, no problem. Yes, it is quite cold. Is this going to help us know what's happening?

Jamie: Yes. Now, **breathe deeply and don't make your abdominal muscles tense.** This is going to be quick, but I need to be able to see what's in there. **Describe the type of pain you've been feeling, please.**

Skyler: Well, **it started as a light pain in the middle of my abdomen, which then moved towards the top right side. It worsened in the last two days, and grew to its peak after I ate.**

Jamie: Any other symptoms?

Skyler: Nausea, vomiting at least twice a day, chest pains... I've also had an excess of gas, more than I've ever had.

Jamie: Understood. **And have you had a fever?**

Skyler: Little, but yes. This has been terrible, and it hasn't allowed me to study for my exams.

Jamie: All right. **Breathe deeply**... now exhale. Inhale once more... exhale again. Oh, I think I see something.

Skyler: What are you seeing? What's going on, doctor?

Jamie: One moment, Skyler. I'm seeing something that may be the cause. Right, I think I know what's happening. This isn't good.

Skyler: You're scaring me, doctor. Please, tell me what's going on.

Jamie: All right. Put your shirt back on and sit here. We have to move fast. This is going to require an emergency surgery. Nothing too serious, but we have to get that out of you.

Skyler: What's wrong with me? What's happening?

Jamie: Well, it seems that **your pain can be due to the serious formation of gallbladder stones**, which are harming you a lot. This problem will continue until it is removed from the root, which is why **I am going to schedule a surgery for today or tomorrow**. It cannot wait past tomorrow, because it could turn into something serious. It could cause your death.

Skyler: It cannot be! Gallbladder stones?! I've never heard of that, what are those about?

Jamie: They are like kidney stones, but these are formed in the gallbladder. One can spend an entire life with a certain amount and size of these stones in the gallbladder without a single symptom, but **it isn't until these begin to crystallize in mass and obstruct the ducts that the problems begin**. In your particular case, **you've already starting to have obstruction**. It is only going to get worse if it isn't operated on.

Skyler: Wow, I see. No wonder I've been feeling so bad. What should I do to prepare myself, then?

Jamie: You must first tell me when you're considering having the surgery. Are you available today? Within three hours, more or less.

Skyler: Yes, it is going to have to be today. I'll tell my mother to bring me clothes and a blanket to sleep with. How long will it take for me to recover from the surgery?

Jamie: It'll be a few weeks, approximately, in which **you'll need complete rest and a no-fat diet**. Are you willing?

Skyler: Yes, as long as it means I'm going to get better. Well, let's get ready for intervention then.

Jamie: Let's go. I'll call the nurse right away.

CONCLUSION

We have reached the end of **Medical Spanish: Real Spanish Medical Conversations for Healthcare Professionals,** but the end of our healthcare stories do not necessarily indicate the end of your Spanish studies!

Each of these short stories, as you may have noticed, were not only written to support you *now,* as you are studying, but will serve greatly as a future reference if (when) you are in a similar situation. After all, what healthcare professional has never had to deal with **a difficult patient, giving bad news** or having to **reanimate a patient?** The value of this textbook hasn't ended now that you've finished reading it; it has only begun.

Nevertheless, we want to provide you with a final set of strategies for you to get the most out of this book and any other materials you may own that are related to the healthcare business. The following is a small list of tasks that will allow you to power your way through Spanish learning and master the language at a medical level — far quicker than any teacher would have been able to provide, that's for sure!

With all of that said, we have now truly reached the end of **Medical Spanish: Real Spanish Medical Conversations for Healthcare Professionals,** and wish you plenty of luck in your future studies. Read the stories as many times as you require, study the vocabulary lists and follow the strategies expressed in this conclusion, and you shall be mastering the Spanish language at a medical level very soon.

Good luck, and don't stop learning — you will be speaking Spanish fluently before you know it!

MORE FROM LINGO MASTERY

Have you been trying to learn Spanish and simply can't find the way to expand your vocabulary?

Do your teachers recommend you boring textbooks and complicated stories that you don't really understand?

Are you looking for a way to learn the language quicker without taking shortcuts?

If you answered *"Yes!"* to at least one of those previous questions, then this book is for you! We've compiled the **2000 Most Common Words in Spanish,** a list of terms that will expand your vocabulary to levels previously unseen.

Did you know that — according to an important study — learning the top two thousand (2000) most frequently used words will enable you to understand up to **84%** of all non-fiction and **86.1%** of fiction literature and **92.7%** of oral speech? Those are *amazing* stats, and this book will take you even further than those numbers!

In this book:

- A detailed introduction with tips and tricks on how to improve your learning
- A list of **2000** of the most common words in Spanish and their translations
- An example sentence for each word – in both Spanish *and* English
- Finally, a conclusion to make sure you've learned and supply you with a final list of tips

Don't look any further, we've got what you need right here!

In fact, we're ready to turn you into a Spanish speaker…

…are you ready to get involved in becoming one?

Do you know what the hardest thing for a Spanish learner is?

Finding PROPER reading material that they can handle...which is precisely the reason we've written this book!

Teachers love giving out tough, expert-level literature to their students, books that present many new problems to the reader and force them to search for words in a dictionary every five minutes — it's not entertaining, useful or motivating for the student at all, and many soon give up on learning at all!

In this book we have compiled 20 easy-to-read, compelling and fun stories that will allow you to expand your vocabulary and give you the tools to improve your grasp of the wonderful Spanish tongue.

How Spanish Short Stories for Beginners works:

- Each story will involve an important lesson of the tools in the Spanish language (Verbs, Adjectives, Past Tense, Giving Directions, and more), involving an interesting and entertaining story with realistic dialogues and day-to-day situations.

- The summaries follow: a synopsis in Spanish and in English of what you just read, both to review the lesson and for you to see if you understood what the tale was about.

- At the end of those summaries, you'll be provided with a list of the most relevant vocabulary involved in the lesson, as well as slang and sayings that you may not have understood at first glance!

- Finally, you'll be provided with a set of tricky questions in Spanish, providing you with the chance to prove that you learned something in the story. Don't worry if you don't know the answer to any — we will provide them immediately after, but no cheating!

We want you to feel comfortable while learning the tongue; after all, no language should be a barrier for you to travel around the world and expand your social circles!

So look no further! Pick up your copy of **Spanish Short Stories for Beginners** and improve your Spanish right now!

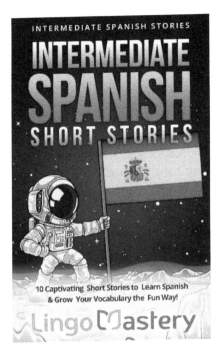

Improve your Spanish skills and grow your vocabulary with these 10 entertaining Spanish short stories!

The best part of learning a new language is experiencing the culture and diving into activities that will enrich your life and vocabulary. The best way to learn a new language is by reading, and in this Spanish book you will find yourself turning page after page to get to the end of each captivating story that will engage your mind and help you improve your Spanish.

In this book you will find:

- **10 captivating short stories** that develop in circumstances such as traveling, personal relationships, among other topics that you will find easy to relate to.

- The stories are broken down into manageable chapters, so you always make progress with the story.

- Carefully written stories with you as an **intermediate level reader in mind**, using straightforward grammar and commonly used words so you can enjoy reading while learning new grammatical structures without being overwhelmed.

- **Plenty of natural dialogues** in each story that you would actually use in an everyday conversation, which will drastically improve your speaking and comprehension ability at the same time!

- At the end of each chapter there will be a comprehensive guide specially designed for intermediate level readers, it will take you through a summary of each story followed by a vocabulary of some of the words from the story to make sure that you understand the story fully.

Chapter by chapter you will find yourself effortlessly reading each story. Not struggling like in basic textbooks or boring reads. You will get involved by reading the dialogue of the characters by learning how to express yourself in different contexts and more importantly by learning new Spanish words that will get you closer to your goal of becoming fully conversational!

Enjoy the book and Buena Suerte!

Is conversational Spanish turning a little too tricky for you? Do you have no idea on how to order a meal or book a room at a hotel?

If your answer to any of the previous questions was 'Yes', then this book is for you!

If there's even been something tougher than learning the grammar rules of a new language, it's finding the way to speak with other people in that tongue. Any student knows this – we can try our best at practicing, but you always want to avoid making embarrassing mistakes or not getting your message through correctly.

'How do I get out of this situation?' many students ask themselves, to no avail, but no answer is forthcoming.

Until now.

We have compiled **MORE THAN ONE HUNDRED** Spanish Stories for Beginners along with their translations, allowing new Spanish speakers to have the necessary tools to begin studying how to set a meeting, rent a car or tell a doctor that they don't feel well! We're not wasting time here with conversations that don't go anywhere: if you want to know how to solve problems (while learning a ton of Spanish along the way, obviously), this book is for you!

How Conversational Spanish Dialogues works:

- Each new chapter will have a fresh, new story between two people who wish to solve a common, day-to-day issue that you will surely encounter in real life.

- A Spanish version of the conversation will take place first, followed by an English translation. This ensures that you fully understood just what it was that they were saying!

- Before and after the main section of the book, we shall provide you with an introduction and conclusion that will offer you important strategies, tips and tricks to allow you to get the absolute most out of this learning material.

- That's about it! Simple, useful and incredibly helpful; you will **NOT** need another conversational Spanish book once you have begun reading and studying this one!

We want you to feel comfortable while learning the tongue; after all, no language should be a barrier for you to travel around the world and expand your social circles!

So look no further!

Pick up your copy of **Conversational Spanish Dialogues** and start learning Spanish right now!

Printed in the USA
CPSIA information can be obtained
at www.ICGtesting.com
LVHW061932270824
789469LV00006B/202